THE BEAT MAKERS

THE UNSUNG HEROES OF THE MERSEY SOUND

ANTHONY HOGAN

AMBERLEY

This book is dedicated to two very special people:

Austin Muscatelli

A warm, friendly, generous, intelligent, and funny man who always pushed and backed me in my writing. I still miss the wind-ups that we would give each other over which Liverpool music club was the most important. I stood strong with my belief in the Iron Door, while Austin would inform me that I needed to be educated in the legend that was Eric's. Of course, it was all in jest and we had mutual respect for one another's taste. The guy who was a 'friend to everyone' left us far too soon, though the memory of his infectious smile and entertaining manner will never leave those who knew and loved him. Rest on bud. COYB.

Valerie Gell

The lead guitarist and second vocalist of the Liverbirds, who we sadly lost during the research of this book. Her insight and belief in music were major contributions to the success of the band that she created with Mary, Sylvia, and Pam. This wonderful, talented, and special lady will remain in our thoughts

First published 2017

Amberley Publishing
The Hill, Stroud
Gloucestershire, GL5 4EP

www.amberley-books.com

British Library Cataloguing in Publication Data.
A catalogue record for this book is available from the British Library.

ISBN 978 1 4456 7208 3 (print)
ISBN 978 1 4456 7209 0 (ebook)

Origination by Amberley Publishing.
Printed in the UK.

Contents

Introduction

The subtitle of this book includes the words 'Unsung Heroes'. Now, I am certain there will be a number of people thinking that Geoff Nugent, Johnny Guitar, Derry Wilkie, and Ted Taylor are hardly unsung, and they would be correct. After all, they are big names who played in big bands of the Mersey music scene. However, they still do not get the credit they fully deserve, and that is why I have made their inclusion. You will also find mention of a number of artists who were also a part of that incredible musical period. A number of those will be well known, yet others may be more obscure. Many will bring back memories, while some will offer a new story to many readers. Whatever the case, I hope that you will enjoy reading about a small section of those who created the music that made the world sit up and take notice.

During the final years of the 1950s, something special began to happen around the Merseyside area: bands began to spring up. Washboards and T-chests were sought after by teenagers, while acoustic guitars became a popular purchase. Of course, it happened elsewhere across the country, but nothing like it did on either side of the River Mersey. Electric guitars, amps, and drums had replaced the household items that had stood in for instruments by the start of the 1960s. Then, something wonderful and truly incredible happened, which would peak with the success of the Beatles.

The Fab Four need no introduction. They remain one of the biggest bands ever to grace the planet and they will crop up as you read through these pages. After all, it is impossible to keep them out, nor would I want to. They have their roots firmly planted within those early years of the Mersey sound. The Beatles, like others, watched their fellow musicians and adapted things to their own style. Many of the people that you will read about here were friends and associates of theirs.

The Beatles went on to worldwide fame, yet they were not the only Mersey artists of that era to find success. Gerry and the Pacemakers had a string of chart hits, with their first three singles 'How Do You Do It', 'I Like It', and 'You'll Never Walk Alone', all reaching the No. 1 spot. Their fourth single, 'I'm The One', made it to the No. 2 position, so they were that close to the quadruple. Their version of 'You'll Never Walk Alone' became an anthem for one of the Merseyside football teams, Liverpool FC. The guys wrote 'Ferry Cross the Mersey', and also featured in the film of the same name. That song has remained very popular, and you can now hear it blasting out from the ferries as they cross the River Mersey.

The Searchers had a number of Top 10 hits, including three No. 1s with 'Sweets For My Sweet', 'Needles and Pins', and 'Don't Throw Your Love Away'. Cilla Black had chart hits up to the mid-1970s, including two No. 1 singles, with 'Anyone Who Had a Heart' and 'You're My World'. The Swinging Blue Jeans took 'Hippy Hippy Shake' to the No. 2 spot and the brilliant 'You're No Good' to No. 3, as well as charting with a number of other singles. The Merseybeats took a number of singles into the charts, with 'I Think of You' selling over a million copies. In 1966 the band split, with Tony Crane and Billy Kinsley forming the duo the Merseys. They had a major hit that same year when they took 'Sorrow' to No. 4 in the UK charts. Billy J. Kramer, backed by the Manchester band the Dakotas, found chart success with a number of Lennon- and McCartney-penned tracks. He had a No. 1 hit with 'Bad To Me', while 'Do You Want To Know a Secret?' and 'I'll Keep You Satisfied' came close to hitting that top spot. 'Little Children' became his second No. 1 in 1964. Lennon and McCartney also provided the Fourmost with two chart hits: 'Hello Little Girl' and 'I'm In Love'. The band also recorded 'A Little Loving', which gave them their highest chart position when it reached No. 6.

The Big Three were one of the most popular bands from Merseyside. They were certainly one of the loudest and produced a pulsating live show. Sadly, their live act did not come across on the singles that they recorded and that was partly down to the choices of the producers. Have a listen to their version of 'What'd I Say' that was recorded at the Cavern Club. It is truly brilliant and will give you a good idea of just how good this band was. Lee Curtis and the All-Stars released a number of singles, though chart success never came their way. They also recorded for the album *Live at the Cavern* and forged out a decent career for themselves in Germany.

The Remo Four were one of the big Mersey sound bands and included the guitarist Colin Manley, who many considered to be the best around. They went on to record a number of singles before releasing a few instrumental songs, including the wonderful 'Peter Gunn'. The band joined up with George Harrison in 1968 to appear on his first solo album *Wonderwall Music*. Earl Preston (George Spruce) probably has the most complicated background of all Merseybeat performers, having fronted so many bands. He was singing his own composed songs on stage before the Beatles had decided to take that route. He also has credit for a number of recordings, though sadly too few for someone with such a superb voice.

Cilla Black was not the only lady of the Mersey sound. There were many talented female performers on the scene who should not be overlooked. As you will see later in this book, the first all-girl rock band grew out of this era. There are some who consider Tiffany and Beryl Marsden to be the finest female vocalists ahead of Cilla. That is, of course, a matter of one's own opinion – though why judge them when you can enjoy them all? Tiffany will appear in the book, while the rumours of a forthcoming biography about Beryl Marsden leaves this author reluctant to detail her too much, hoping that her long-awaited story will finally be here for us all to enjoy in the not-too-distant future. Beryl was, and still is, an incredible vocalist.

Many other Mersey sound bands and singers have recorded singles that have made or hovered around the outside of the UK charts. Others were recorded without recognition, while a number found a favourable outcome with their singles in other countries. A few local musicians and singers went on to play with some of the biggest bands around. Many became backing and some turned to production. Performers from that incredible Mersey sound era have gone on to become actors, comedians, DJs, radio presenters, TV personalities, session, musicians, producers, writers, painters – you name it and they have probably done it. They really were/are a talented bunch of people who played a part in an incredible chapter of musical history.

Producing a book that is based upon such a diverse subject was never going to be easy. The Mersey sound era did not finish with those wonderful early bands and singers; it went on until the late 1960s, as the area produced talent after talent. Clearly, some artists from the era are either not going to receive a mention or will not be recalled as much as others. It may leave a number upset to discover that their favourites have not been included. I can only apologise about this, though including everyone would have been a daunting task. I have chosen a variety of people who will hopefully interest the reader. My hope is that this book will go some small way to gaining the recognition that the artists from this most wonderful of periods fully deserve. These are the people who made the beat, and changed music as we know it.

1

Geoff Nugent

Geoff Nugent was born 'Gordon Geoffrey Nugent' on 23 February 1943 at No. 9a Speke Road in Garston, Liverpool. His father was Robert Nugent, who was born in 1907 and worked as a fitter in an aircraft factory. It is said that there was not anything that Robert did not know about planes. His mother was Amy Davies. Robert and Amy had married in Liverpool in 1932. The family moved to No. 29 Marton Green in Speke when Gordon was still a young boy. His brothers kept telling him that Gordon was a 'poncey' name and that he should use Geoff. So he did.

Geoff, with his rather good soprano voice, joined the school choir. When he was aged nine he was spotted singing at the Dunlop factory Christmas party (where his parents worked) and was offered the opportunity to sing a song on the popular radio programme *Workers Playtime*. He agreed, and proudly sang the Jim Reeves song 'Bimbo' to workers around the country.

Aged around ten, Geoff entered a competition for a chance to meet Roy Rogers and his horse Trigger. Geoff won the competition and was invited over to America. However, his parents said that they could not take the time off work or afford to go with him, so he never went. When Roy Rogers came to perform his show at the Liverpool Empire theatre in March 1954, Geoff was contacted and invited along. During the show, Geoff sat on Trigger and held Rogers' guns. He was speechless and later said that it was a most fabulous time for a little boy.

Geoff showed an interest towards music at an early age. He took piano lessons, but when his brother Bobby gave him his Hohner President guitar when he was aged around eleven he was hooked on the instrument. His mother would ask 'what about the piano?'

and Bobby would reply 'well he can't take a piano on the bus can he mum?' Later, he bought a new guitar from Rushworth's and had to have his father sign the papers for the hire purchase. His father was astounded at the price of the guitar and said that he could have bought a Mini cheaper.

When Geoff's family moved to Speke from Garston he became very good friends with a boy named George Harrison. George lived in Upton Green, just over the road from where Geoff lived. The two boys were friends from the age of around twelve. Geoff's birthday was 23 February, and George, back then, thought that his birthday was 24 February. It was actually recorded on his birth certificate as 25 February, but as George was born close to midnight on the 24th he had thought that day as his birthday.

Geoff would say having George for a friend was great, as he came to his birthday then Geoff went to his the day after. He would recall running over the fields in Speke with George and other friends. They would both practise their guitars together in each other's houses. Sometimes they would both sit on the wall of a neighbour's house and flatten the privet hedges by leaning into them while playing their guitars. The local kids would come and watch as they played. They also went to the houses of friends to play and sing. This is the way that Geoff and George first learned to do what they did best.

In 1957, Geoff formed a skiffle group with his friends Dave Kehoe and Brian Foy called the Rhythm Rockers, who played at a number of venues around the Garston area, including Wilson Hall. Geoff's mother bought him a small Alnico amplifier that cost her almost a week's wages. George Harrison turned up at Geoff's house and asked if he could borrow it for an audition with a band called the Quarrymen. George was known for returning borrowed items in a worse state than he had received them, so Geoff refused to lend him the amp. Friend or no friend, he knew his mother would go mad if anything happened to the amp.

Geoff's brother Bobby bought two tickets for the Buddy Holly concert at the Philharmonic Hall on 20 March 1958. Geoff bunked off school so that he could go to the show. He never told his mum or dad as he knew that they would never let him go to another one. Geoff was a huge fan of Buddy Holly and he also liked country music, with his favourite performer being Hank Williams.

Geoff took his guitar with him when the family went on holiday to the Isle of Man in 1958. There is a well-known photograph of him playing it while walking along a street in Douglas with a number of young girls following behind. After returning from holiday, Geoff went out to the Holyoake Hall on Smithdown Road. The hall DJ, Bob Wooler, suggested that he do a few songs with the band, who were playing that evening as Bob Evans and the Five Shillings. Geoff sang 'Teenager In Love' and 'Dream Lover'. The band were impressed and asked him to join them. Geoff agreed and teamed up with Bob Evans (drums), Billy Evans (bass), Les Maguire (sax/piano), Mike Millwood (rhythm guitar), and a lad called Ike who played lead guitar. Ike was soon replaced by Peter Cook. Chris Huston came in to replace Cook on lead guitar as the guys settled into rehearsing and performing to hone their skills. They went down well on the local circuit as they turned into a decent rocking band. Geoff took a job in Tithebarn Street with a company who made prosthesis limbs. With a regular wage, he could save to buy himself better musical equipment.

A name change in 1959 saw the band become the Vegas Five, before a local newspaper misprint set the scene for the emergence of one Merseyside's biggest bands. The lads had been booked to play a gig at Litherland Town Hall, which was advertised in the *Liverpool Echo*. Somehow, the 'What's On' and 'Obituary' sections of the newspaper became mixed up during printing. So, down as playing at the club that night were 'Undertakers' instead of the Vegas Five. The band was encouraged to use the name and became Bob's Undertakers, then the Undertakers. As a gimmick, they would walk on stage to the sounds of the 'Funeral March'.

In 1961, Les Maguire left the band to become the keyboard player with Gerry and the Pacemakers. Brian Jones now joined the Undertakers on sax. Dave Cooper was on bass, and Jimmy McManus took lead vocals. When Bob Evans decided to leave the band he was replaced by Warren (Bugs) Pemberton. Bugs, who had been drumming with Dee and the Dynamites, suggested that they recruit his former band member, Jackie Lomax, when Dave Cooper left. Jackie was a rhythm guitarist, but was asked to play bass. He had never played one before but he soon took to it. The band soon noticed that Jackie had an amazing voice. Their singer, Jimmy McManus, had been picking fights with audience members. This was no good for the band so they dropped him and made Jackie the lead singer. We now had the classic five Undertakers: Geoff, Chris, Brian, Jackie and Bugs. All the lads were from Wallasey, apart from Geoff, who was from the other side of the River Mersey.

The Undertakers. (Courtesy of Mave Atherton and Christopher Huston)

The guys hit the ground running. In a very short time they had established themselves as one of the top Merseyside bands. They played the main venues including the Aintree Institute, the Lathom, and Litherland Town Hall among others. They played the Tower Ballroom in New Brighton on 17 May of 1962 alongside Jerry Lee Lewis. Others appearing on the show were the Big Three, Kingsize Taylor and the Dominoes, Billy Kramer, Derry Wilkie and the Pressmen, and Vince Earl and the Zeros. However, it was at the Iron Door Club that they really took off. The band played the Iron Door almost every week and became one of the most sought-after acts there by the paying public. Their following became huge – and why not? Not only were they a great band, but they also entertained the audiences with their thumping stage show and gimmicks. Brian Jones worked as a butcher and would come on stage armed with sheep's eyeballs. During a song, he would slap one onto his forehead so he looked as if he had three eyes. The crowd loved this, and the girls would all try to catch the eyeballs that he threw into the crowd, before slapping them onto their own foreheads. Their signature song was 'Mashed Potatoes' and they were certain to get an audience bouncing along with them when they performed it. The Undertakers would bounce and stomp their feet together in time during a song. They were an exciting and brilliant band who gained a great deal of popularity on the local scene.

On 7 August 1962, the Undertakers took to the stage at the Star-Club in Hamburg for a two-week stint. Their time in Germany was a great success and they returned home a better band. On 9 October they made their debut at the Cavern Club. There is a famous photograph of the queue outside the Cavern Club stretching the length of Mathew Street. It is often claimed that the people in the queue were waiting to watch the Beatles perform. Simply, that is untrue. The Undertakers were, in fact, playing at the Cavern and the queue was full of people waiting to see them perform. This is how popular the band was. Beryl Marsden would often sing with them during this period.

Their popularity on both sides of the Mersey continued, and it did not go unnoticed. Brian Epstein contacted the band with an offer to manage them. The lads turned him down as they had already signed up with Ralph Webster, who ran the Orrell Park Ballroom and a number of other venues across the city. He could ensure the band constant work, while Epstein was the guy that they bought records from. John Lennon told them that 'Eppy' has done nothing for the Beatles, and that was enough for the Undertakers to drop any thoughts of jumping ship from Ralph. Of course, pretty soon Brian had the Beatles on a path to huge stardom.

The guys were back in Hamburg at the Star-Club on 7 January 1963. They appeared here for a month's stint before returning to the UK and signing a recording contract with Pye Records. Tony Hatch was assigned to produce them. After studio work and touring, they went back to Hamburg and the Star-Club. They performed at the club for a month from 20 June, and once again thrilled the people who came to watch them play.

By the time the band arrived back home their first single had been released. The guys had wanted their fans' favourite song 'Mashed Potatoes' to be the A-side, but Hatch relegated it to a B-side and chose instead 'Everybody Loves a Lover'. The song did not sell well and never managed to make the charts. That same summer, Geoff married his partner, Veronica Collins, in the Prescot area of Liverpool. On 17 August the band appeared on the TV programme *Thank Your Lucky Stars* alongside Val Doonican and Chubby Checker.

They were approached to take part in the 1963 TV documentary *The Mersey Sound*. The Undertakers were filmed playing at the Iron Door Club. They wore their top hats and long coats and bounced along in unison as they played 'Mashed Potatoes'. The guys had great fun recording for the show. Incidentally, the Beatles were filmed for the documentary while playing at the Little Theatre in Southport, where they played to an empty theatre with the show dubbing on a screaming audience.

In September 1963, the Undertakers released their second single with Pye. Tony Hatch again insisted on choosing the A-side and opted for 'What About Us'. The B-side 'Money' was the song that the guys had wanted but were overruled. Once again the single failed to hit the charts, leaving the band annoyed by the situation. Hatch was a good producer, he just had no idea how to utilise the Undertakers.

For their third single with Pye, the Undertakers were finally allowed to choose what songs should be recorded. They chose 'Just a Little Bit' as the A-side, with 'Stupidity' on the reverse. The single sold well, no world beater, but it did get them into the charts at No. 49. On 22 February 1964, the band once more appeared on *Thank Your Lucky Stars*. Other guests on the show included Billy J. Kramer and the Dakotas, and Dusty Springfield. Not long after, Geoff and Veronica were blessed with their first child, and life was good for the happy couple.

The Undertakers went on a short tour of Scotland at the end of June 1964. In early July, Geoff and the guys were enjoying the sunshine by a loch in the countryside. They had bought air rifles to entertain themselves and were firing them into the water. Jackie Lomax, who had been sunbathing, stood up as Chris Huston fired his gun and was shot in the back of his neck. A mad dash to Paisley took place, where Jackie had the slug removed in hospital.

With Jackie recovered, the band went out for a tour of Germany in September. During a visit to East Berlin, Chris and Brian were arrested for bringing in East German money and, believe it or not, Monopoly money. They were held overnight before they were released back into the western sector of the city.

The band's fourth single 'If You Don't Come Back' had been released in September of 1964, accompanied on the B-side by 'Think'. Pye had insisted that the band shorten their name to the Takers' for this single, claiming that 'Undertakers' was putting buyers off. There weren't enough copies printed for sale as the pressing plant was on its annual leave, so the single had no chance of success. The guys had had enough of the name changing and messing around with recordings so they ended their contract with Pye. It is such a shame that they were never given a fair chance at recording as they had such a talent that should have been used in the correct way.

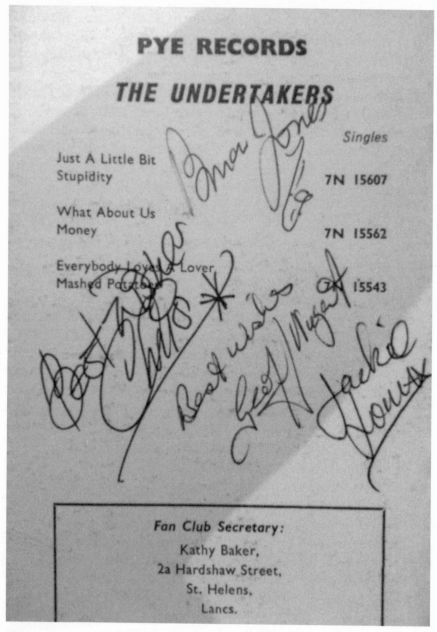

The Undertakers' promotional card, signed by all members except Bugs. (Courtesy of Mave Atherton)

The band played around Merseyside and a number of tours across the country during 1965. On 26 July they played a benefit gig at the Cavern Club. Twelve bands performed to raise money for charity including the Clayton Squares, the Escorts, the Spinners, Steve Aldo, the Scaffold, and Hank Walters. Without a recording contract, the lads were considering their options as to what direction they should move the band. The Undertakers successfully replied to an advert seeking British bands for work in America. They took the opportunity and prepared to fly out. However, they would have to do it without Geoff as he had no desire to leave his wife and young son at home to travel so far away. He informed the guys that he would be staying in Liverpool and wished them well. The band flew out to New York and Geoff moved into 1966 considering the options for his future.

Geoff decided to take up a solo career under the name Verne Gordon and soon had a residency at the Grafton. He also performed with a number of singing groups, one that included Joan Chisholm and Sandra Collins. By the 1970s he had taken employment as a performer aboard the *Queen Elizabeth 2* cruise ship and his time there provided a number or stories.

One time, when *Queen Elizabeth 2* had docked in New York, Geoff was eager to find a music shop so that he could buy some new guitar strings. The crew were warned not to leave the ship alone as the district they were near was considered dangerous. Urgent need for the strings was enough for Geoff to decide that it was a risk worth taking, and off he went in search of a taxi. However, the passengers had all by now left to explore the city and everywhere was deserted. Geoff walked along the dockside until he spotted a wide road and headed towards it. Hardly any traffic was coming along but he thought he would follow it. After a while, he saw a man in the distance and, as he neared him, Geoff asked if he knew where a music store was or a taxi rank. The guy looked at him for a few seconds and said 'You're Geoff Nugent from the Undertakers. I used to watch you at the Orrell Park Ballroom'. The guy then gave a whistle and a cab arrived from nowhere. He spoke to the driver, then beckoned Geoff to get in. He was taken to a music shop and the driver waited for him while he made his purchase, before taking him back to the ship. When Geoff tried to pay, the driver refused to take any money from him. Geoff never found out who that guy was who sorted out the taxi for him that day.

During one of his days off in New York, he fancied a walk and set off for a stroll only to lose his direction and find himself lost. He chose to keep on walking and found himself wandering through an area where many black people lived. It started to dawn on Geoff that he

The 1970s snap of Geoff that always made him laugh. (Courtesy of the Geoff Nugent Collection)

had no idea how safe the place was and that maybe he should not be there. He noticed three men sitting on the steps of a house and went over to ask them for directions. One of the guys said 'you're a Limey' (a Brit), then they all shook hands with Geoff before inviting him into the house where he had a great afternoon with them. So much for being worried about the area.

The arrival of the *Queen Elizabeth 2* in New York saw the departure of a number of musicians who had played alongside Geoff on the trip out. They were off to join the Count Basie orchestra at the Jack Dempsey Club. They informed the crew to come along and watch them play at the club the next time that the ship docked in New York. Of course, on their next stop a number of them took up the offer and headed off to the club. They were shown to a table and sat back to enjoy the show. During the performance, the band announced that in the audience that evening was the resident *Queen Elizabeth 2* singer, Geoff Nugent, who they would now like to invite up on stage to perform a number with them. Geoff was absolutely stunned but eagerly made his way up. He grabbed the microphone and said 'In the key of C and follow me', and he and the band burst into song. Geoff was delighted by this experience and would later comment that it was the most outstanding time of his life. He was very humbled by it and felt it an honour and a privilege to have sung with the Count Basie orchestra. With the tours aboard the *Queen Elizabeth 2* over, Geoff returned to Liverpool, where he continued to perform. He had formed a new version of the Undertakers with Brian Jones and they brought those wonderful sounds of the early 1960s back to life.

One day during the 1970s, Geoff was using an electric saw while doing some DIY when it slipped and almost severed the top of a finger on his left hand. He wrapped it and went straight to hospital, where he was seen by a consultant who recognised him as he had booked him to play at his daughter's twenty-first birthday. The finger was reattached and bandaged and Geoff was informed that how it healed would determine whether it could be saved. He could not play the guitar, yet that did not stop him getting up on a stage to sing with his hand strapped to his chest. One night while on stage his hand took a knock and he returned to the hospital, where he saw the same consultant. The news was bad and amputation was the only outcome. Geoff asked if all of the finger could be removed – right down to the knuckle – to give him a chance of being able to play the guitar. It was agreed and the operation was done. Again, with a bandaged hand, he continued to sing on stage. During one gig the guitarist in the band took ill and had to be taken from the stage. With nobody available to step in, Geoff removed his bandages and managed to improvise his way through the remainder of the set. From then on he played every moment that he could. Of course, he could no longer shape the chords as he once had, though he found ways to play them with just three fingers. Basically, Geoff retrained himself to play, which is pretty remarkable dedication.

Geoff was a founder member of the Merseycats charity, which helped local children. He also served a term on the committee as chairman. He appeared at many of the Merseybeat-based concerts and events that took place. He must have played with almost every band that took to a stage, but that was Geoff – he loved the music. Everything changed when Veronica became ill. Geoff put the music aside to nurse his wife during an illness that would sadly claim her life in early 2006. It was the music that helped him cope with this devastating event, and he threw himself into it.

Geoff continued to play a solo act as well as with the Undertakers. They performed around the country and at special events such as the Mathew Street festivals, Merseybeat gigs, and anniversary concerts at home and abroad. Whenever Jackie Lomax was over from the USA he would team up with the band as they thrilled the crowds. On 20 March 2008, Geoff had another proud moment when the Undertakers appeared at the Buddy Holly tribute night at the Philharmonic Hall in Liverpool, fifty years to the day since schoolboy Geoff had watched his idol perform at the hall. Geoff was so honoured to play at this event and his only sadness was that his brother Bobby, who lived in Australia, was not there to watch him.

Jackie Lomax and Geoff Nugent. (Courtesy of Mave Atherton)

The year 2008 also saw Geoff proudly being made an ambassador for Liverpool's capital of culture. He joined the Merseyrats charity, with whom he would compère their Thursday night events every week, while performing himself and making sure the bands were on and off stage on time. There's a funny story told about Geoff playing at one gig: an old guy who was well into his eighties shouted, 'Is that young Geoff up there on the stage?' Geoff was sixty-eight at the time.

In 2010, Geoff and Mave Atherton flew to Pittsburgh to visit their friends Susie Barbour and Rich Dugan. While there, their friends drove them all the way to Tennessee to visit Christopher Huston. They drove via Louisville, Kentucky, where they stayed the night to attend the Abbey Road on the River festival. Geoff was invited on stage by the Elliotts and gladly accepted the invitation to perform a few numbers. They also bumped into Terry Sylvester from the Escorts while they were here. Then it was on to see Chris; both he and Geoff were delighted to spend a few days together.

Geoff had recorded a number of studio tracks from 2010 onwards. In 2011 he showed his love for country music when he released the CD album *The Country Side of Me*, which proved very popular across Merseyside. On 13 April 2012, Geoff, Jackie and Brian performed as the Undertakers at the Kaiserkeller club in Hamburg for the fifty-year

Chris Huston and Geoff Nugent in Tennessee. (Courtesy of Mave Atherton)

anniversary celebrations of the Star-Club. They were thrilled by the gig as fans queued to see them and they spent a while signing autographs and posing for photos. On 15 September 2013, Geoff and the guys were hit with the tragic news that Jackie Lomax had died during a visit home to the Wirral. Within weeks, on 13 October, Bugs Pemberton passed away in Los Angeles. Brian, Chris, and Geoff were devastated by the loss of their former bandmates and the music scene was much poorer for it.

The Undertakers had agreed to play at the Kaiserkeller's 55th anniversary celebrations in Hamburg on 17 October 2014 and were really looking forward to it. Plans were in place, with hotels and flights booked. Tragically, the gig was never played, as Geoff passed away on 12 October. His family, friends, fellow musicians and fans were stunned and saddened by the loss of this popular man. He was a wonderful and talented guy who did so much for so many and was a friend of everyone he met.

In tribute to Geoff, a limited edition CD album of his studio recordings was released in 2015 called *Geoff Nugent – My Life*. It featured twenty songs that Geoff had put down in the previous few years. It also showed us the talent of the man who loved to perform and entertain.

Brian Jones said of Geoff:

The first time that I saw Geoff was when my mother opened the door to him after he knocked at my house one day. He piped up with 'does Brian Jones live here?' to which mum replied, 'who are you?' He threw back the answer 'I'm Geoff Nugent. I want to know if Brian will join our band.' I then leaned over mum's shoulder and said, 'yes! I will join'. I had been a singer but explained to Geoff that I had bought a saxophone and was taking lessons. The sax was not a problem and I was now in the band. At first, I stood at the back during gigs playing one or two notes every now and again until I had learned the instrument and was able to produce a decent sound. Geoff was a diamond, a truly lovely man. In Geoff, Bugs, and Jackie, I lost three of my best mates in just over a year. I miss them all terribly.

Christopher Huston said,

It is impossible to separate the guys. Dear Geoff, Jackie and Bugs, they were our brothers. Who could have known, way back then, when we started playing music, that the paths of our lives would take us to so many places and the opportunity to do so many creative and exciting

Johnny 'Guitar' Byrne and Geoff Nugent in the Montrose Club, Liverpool. You can see Geoff's missing finger on his left hand. (Courtesy of Mave Atherton)

things. In the beginning, we couldn't afford the musical instruments or the fancy clothes that we saw the US artists wearing, and we didn't see ourselves doing the equally fancy footwork that they did, so we stamped our feet for excitement. It wouldn't have - couldn't have - been the same without Jackie, Bugs, Brian, Geoff and myself. I've got all four of them to be forever thankful to for the fabulous times that we shared, which in turn led to the wonderfully creative life that I have been fortunate to have led. Geoff was an integral part of the band in that he both played and sang, as did both Brian and Jackie. As such, during our sets Geoff, who had a great voice, would do several songs, which gave Jackie, who was our de facto lead singer a break and this also served to add variety to our performances. Add that he was also an important part of the rhythm section of the group, keeping it solid and consistent. The camaraderie that the group had was wonderful, as it brought out both the best and worst in all of us. I mean, how can you expect to be on the road for as long as we were and not get into differences of opinion and arguments. The fact that there were no out-n-out fights says a lot. Geoff, in retrospect, had a wonderful personality in that he was 'on stage' much of the time. By that, I mean that he was a natural showman, and he was excitable and fun to be with. In spite of everything, we all made it through the years that we were together. Geoff continued to be the talented and natural showman that he was.

A number of years back, Geoff decided that he wanted to put his story down in words. He wrote a little but never got around to doing

Geoff Nugent being interviewed by German TV in Hamburg. (Courtesy of Mave Atherton)

anything with it. There really is only one way to end this chapter and that is by letting Geoff finish it himself with his own story. Nothing has been changed or corrected, this is how he wrote it. Thank you for everything Geoff, over to you.

Geoff's Story

Where do I begin?

I suppose it all started when I was seven years of age. My Mum sent me for piano lessons, which I studied for about eighteen months. I loved to sing as well. I was always singing around the house. Then my eldest brother Bobby bought a guitar home. He showed me my first three chords on the guitar and I was totally hooked! Much to my undoing, I gave up the piano and Mum was not pleased. Bobby said, 'Mum he can carry a guitar, he can't carry a piano!' So the guitar became my life from that day onwards.

I started senior school and we had a music teacher called Pop Hayes who was a great jazz player on piano. Pop helped me tremendously in my early days. He was a great inspiration to me and I think Pop Hayes encouraged me as he knew I wanted to make my future in music.

Both my parents encouraged me in everything I did. I was asked to play at Dunlop's kid's Christmas Party and little did I know at that time, that BBC were studying to make a program for 'Worker's Playtime'. My parents were approached for me to do a spot. I was so excited to be taking part in such a well-known radio program at that time. I sang 'BIMBO' the Jim Reeves hit and felt a bit overwhelmed with all the attention. This was in my school dinner hour and it was a bit of a let down when I had to return to school for the afternoon session.

The guitar became part of me. Around the same time I met George Harrison. We lived a road apart in Speke and we used to visit each others houses a few times a week. George became a familiar face at my house. My Mum used to feed us and gave us fry ups. George always liked the skin off the rice pudding and my two older brothers would want to know where the skin had gone and which of us had eaten it. George and I played our guitars, which were both the same (no names on them) and we'd play on the street corners in Speke. George's birthday was one day after mine. He would play Happy Birthday to You on his guitar and the next day I'd do the same for him.

George and I attended different schools. George went to the Liverpool Institute and met Paul McCartney on the bus on the way there and the rest is history. We still met, but not quite as much as we had done. I went to the local Secondary School. I joined a skiffle group when I was fourteen with lads from Scouts, Dave Kehoe and Brian Foy, we were occasionally joined by Dave's sister Chris Kehoe who later on became a member of the Littlewood's Songsters. We played local church venues and OAP's clubs.

I even took my guitar on holiday to the Isle of Man when I was fifteen. There is a picture of me playing my guitar walking along a street in Douglas, with a few pretty girls following me. The Saturday night on my return from holiday I went out to the Hollyoak Ballroom in Smithdown Road. There was a band playing called Bob Evans and the Five Shillings. The D.J. at that time was Bob Wooler. Bob had heard me sing at the Wilson Hall in Garston with The Rhythm Rockers and asked me if I would sing with the Five Shillings. I sang two songs, 'Teenager in Love' and 'Dream Lover'. Bob Evans asked me if I would like to join the band. From The Five Shillings it went to The Vegas Five, which consisted of Dave 'Mushy' Cooper, Jimmy McManus, Chris Huston, Bob Evans and myself.

We should have been appearing on the Litherland Town Hall one evening in early 1960 and the Liverpool Echo made an error with the billing and we were billed as THE UNDERTAKERS. The Vegas Five were somewhere in the OBITS and The Undertakers were born. Our regular venues were at The Litherland Town Hall, The Craftman's Ellesmere Port, The Kings Club, The Orrell Park Ballroom, The River Park in Chester, The Plaza St Helens and our Favourite The Iron Door. We played the Cavern lunch time sessions and evenings, as all the local groups did. We were voted one of the top ten popular bands in Liverpool

I have met and played with some of the most famous and remarkable people in my career, who became my lifelong friends. I played The Star Club in Hamburg in the early days with The Beatles, Tony Sheridan, Roy Young, Bill Haley, Little Richard, Jerry Lee Lewis, Joey Dee and the Starlighters, Wee Willie Harris, Kingsize Taylor and the Dominos, Lee Curtis and the All Stars, Screaming Lord Sutch, Gerry & The Pacemakers, Ian & The Zodiacs, The Swingin' Blue Jeans, Rory Storm & the Hurricanes, Cliff Bennett & the Rebel Rousers, Johnny Kidd & The Pirates, The Rattles with Klaus Voorman. Astrid Kerscher was our photographer as well and she became famous for the early Beatles pictures.

None of this would have been possible without the band and my great musician pals, 'The Undertakers' then and now, especially now, it's forty-five years on we're still Rockin' and the beat goes on.

2

Derry Wilkie

Derry Wilkie was born on 10 January 1941 in Liverpool to John Wilkie and Grace Walker. A number of sources state that his real name was Derek Davis. However, this is incorrect and he really was Derry Wilkie, or, to give him his full birth name, Richard Derry Wilkie. His father John (known as Jack) was born in Nigeria, and was a merchant seaman who could play the mandolin. His mother, Grace, had been born in Liverpool. She had a beautiful voice and many of her friends considered her talented enough to have been a jazz singer. Grace's father had come from Liberia. Derry was the second eldest of nine children and grew up in the Toxteth area, living in Upper Stanhope Street, Upper Parliament Street, Berkley Street, and Kent Gardens. There is a little confusion about which early school he attended, with a number of people saying they knew him at Harrington Boarding School, which was situated near to Cains Brewery at the bottom of Stanhope Street, while others claim he was a classmate of theirs at Windsor Street juniors. Of course, he possibly – and probably – attended both of these schools. For certain, he later went to St James Secondary Modern on the corner of St James Road and Alfred Street. Derry did a bit of boxing at school and he also loved to sing. Happily, he would give a song whenever the opportunity arose.

The White House pub on the corner of Duke Street/Berry Street, once had a lounge attached to the property. On a Sunday afternoon when the pubs closed at 3 p.m., the lounge would open and be full to the brim. Many musicians would come along and a huge jamming session would take place, with anyone who wanted to play or sing a few songs accommodated. Derry and his friends would visit to sing even though they were too young to be in a pub. It was like a training ground to them as they gained the experience of performing in front

Derry Wilkie as a young boy. (Courtesy of the Wilkie family collection)

of an audience. Derry's friend and fellow singer, Sugar Deen, recalled these early days: 'Derry was brilliant. He would wave his arms as he sang and danced and the people watching would join in with him. I would ask Derry if I could sing before him as he was a nightmare to follow as he was so talented.'

In 1959, Derry was introduced to a group by the name of the Hy-Tones, who were very impressed with him and offered him a job as their singer. He accepted, and so began a musical career that would span almost forty years. The band consisted of Howie Casey (sax), Billy Hughes (guitar), Brian Griffiths (guitar), Stan Johnson (guitar), Jimmy O'Connor (bass and vocals), Stan Foster (piano), Derek Gill (drums) and, of course, Derry as lead vocalist. They would practice in the front room of Brian Griffith's house. One of their first performance saw them win a music competition at the Holyoake Hall, Smithdown Road.

Early in 1959, Derry had married Evangeline Welch (known as Eve) at a registry office in the city. In November 1959, Derry and Eve were blessed with the birth of their first child.

The band changed its name to Derry Wilkie and the Seniors. Derek Gill was replaced by Jeff Wallington on drums, while Paul Whitehead took over from Jimmy O'Connor on bass. The group went down well and gained a loyal following. Derry has been described as a brilliant performer whose stage show was absolutely electric. He was a fantastic dancer and brought this talent up on stage with him. When introduced at a gig, he would not just walk onto a stage and start singing, he was a showman and his show began before the songs did. Often, as the band started to play their music, Derry would come from the back of the audience and creep through them in an over-exaggerated slow-motion walk. He would climb onto and walk upon any tables, chairs, or benches that were in the way of him and the stage. By the time that he had the microphone in his hand he had whipped the crowd up into excitement and had them in the palm of his hand – all this, of course, without singing a single note.

Derry managed to get the band a few gigs in the Beacon Club on Parliament Street, which was run by the former boxer Joey Bygraves. They also played at times during the intervals at the Rialto cinema/ballroom on Upper Parliament Street. Derry could also dance, and won a dance competition at the Rialto with his dance partner, Iris Cole.

The band became regulars at the Jacaranda club in Slater Street, a club owned by Allan Williams. Williams had arranged for Gene

Derry Wilkie. (Courtesy of Peter Kaye Photography)

Vincent to play at the Liverpool stadium on 3 May 1960. Derry and the boys were booked to play on the bill and were full of excitement by the experience. London impresario Larry Parnes attended the concert and was so impressed by the Liverpool bands that appeared on the show that he asked Williams to arrange an audition the following week as he wanted some of the local groups to back the singers under his management on tours. On 10 May, the Seniors played the audition at the Wyvern club in Seel Street. Mr Parnes and Billy Fury, one of his star products, thought highly of the band and they were offered a season in Blackpool backing Duffy Power. The lads were delighted and all gave their day jobs up. However, Duffy had to pull out of the season due to personal reasons. The Seniors had their contracts cancelled and turned on Williams to complain. To calm them down, he promised to take them to the 2i's coffee bar in Old Crompton Street, Soho, London, which was a haven for talent spotters and promoters.

Williams, true to his word, took the guys to London. As they played, a German club owner, Bruno Koschmider, approached Williams and began chatting to him. Bruno had come over to find an English band to play at his club in Hamburg called the Kaiserkeller. He was very impressed with the Seniors and taken by Derry's lively performance. The guys were offered a contract at the German club and took it up. Derry now had to go home and inform Evangeline that he was going to work away for three months. She would be looking after their baby while he was away, but she did not stand in his way so Derry prepared to leave.

The guys arrived in Hamburg in July 1960 for their residency at the Kaiserkeller, but not after some trouble at the border. Their train was stopped and the police came aboard and asked the band for work permits. They had none, of course, and said that they were tourists. The police looked at the instruments, and then threw them off the train. Panic phone calls were made to Bruno in Hamburg, who managed to get them safely to the club. The promised permits, however, never arrived. They found Hamburg to be a far cry from Liverpool as they settled into a punishing routine of playing up to six hours a night in a club located in the heart of Hamburg's red-light district. It was a real eye-opener for the boys, but they loved it.

Their living quarters were an absolute joke, with the lads having to share two rooms next to the ladies toilets. Derry slept on a couch, while the others tried to make themselves some kind of bed from what they could find. One small basin in the ladies toilet was all that they had to wash with. In the early hours the management would lock the guys in the club until the following afternoon, though they were all asleep during that period anyway.

The crowds at the club loved them and Bruno would shout at them to 'mach schau' ('make show'). This was to draw in the punters from outside and Derry could be relied on to mach schau all around the stage. When they heard that Allan Williams was sending the Beatles out to play for Bruno, the band told him that sending out a group like them would ruin the set-up for everyone else. You have to remember that at this time the Beatles were still way down the pecking order of Liverpool's top bands. However, they did come out in August and played at the nearby Indra club. At the end of September, Rory Storm and the Hurricanes arrived to take over from the Seniors at the Kaiserkeller. When they saw their living conditions they decided to book into a seaman's mission. Mind you, the Beatles were living in an even worse place in the Bambi Kino cinema.

When their contract was up the Seniors decided to stay in Hamburg for a while longer. Some of the guys played backing for strippers in a local club, while Derry found work singing with a German Dixieland band. Peter Eckhorn had offered them work at the Top Ten Club, but when he found out that they had no permits or visas he told them to get themselves to the British Embassy and sort them out. The staff there took their passports from them and had the guys returned to England.

The band began playing the local venues once more. In fact, their first gig back was strangely enough at a newly opened club called the Top Ten. They played there a few times until a local gang decided that they were taking it over. They arrived mob-handed and chased away the bouncers before setting their sights on the band, who happened to be the Seniors. Derry waded in and soon left a number of gang members lying around the floor. Just as the lads were being overpowered the police arrived and the gang ran off. The guys had been storing their gear at the club and one night it caught fire. Clearly, it was something to do with the gang. Everything was destroyed: all their instruments and equipment. The guys were so downhearted that they decided to call it a day. However, by January 1961 they had reformed. Billy Hughes, Stan Foster, and Jeff Wallington departed, so Derry, Howie, Brian and Paul carried on the band and brought in Frank Wibberley on drums and Freddie Fowell as a second vocalist. Freddie would later go on to find fame as a comedian under the name of Freddie Starr.

Sadly, Derry experienced racism from people who were clearly jealous that a black man had more talent and popularity than them. It is to his credit that Derry shrugged it off and continued to do what he did best. The Seniors played the local area for a few months before Freddie Fowell announced that he had been given a recording contract audition with Fontana. Freddie informed Fontana that he was in a band and they agreed to audition them all. The lads travelled

Derry Wilkie promotional picture. (Courtesy of the Wilkie family collection)

to London, passed their audition, and were signed to Fontana. On 15 December 1961 they played at the Tower Ballroom in New Brighton. On the show with them were the Beatles, Rory Storm and the Hurricanes, and the Big Three, who were joined by Brian Casser to reform for one night only as Cass and the Cassanovas.

Rita Martelli was a good friend of Derry and spoke about how he helped her gain access to one of the most popular clubs in Liverpool.

Derry was a friend in the 60s. The Blue Angel was the club to go to as all
the bands and many visiting stars went there after their gigs. I tried many
times to join and was always knocked back. On yet another of these nights
I bumped into Derry. He said, 'what's wrong with your face?' When I told
him he said, 'come with me' and he signed me in and I promptly joined!

The band travelled back to London to record an album for Fontana.
The company asked them to change their name to Howie Casey
and the Seniors, and the guys agreed. They also wanted the songs to
follow the latest dance craze of 'The Twist', so the lads got to work
writing a number of songs there and then. Derry co-wrote 'Double
Twist' with Freddie Fowell, and also composed 'Big Daddie' and 'Bone
Shakin Annie' for the album. They recorded everything in just one
afternoon session. The title of the album was *Twist at the Top* and it
featured a lady performing twist dance moves on the cover. Twelve
songs were to be found on the disc. In February 1962 the album
was released, along with a single that featured 'Double Twist' on the
A-side and 'True Fine Mama' on the reverse. This made them the first
Merseyside beat band to record either a single or an album.

Part of their contract with Fontana had them signed to an agency
who would find them work. They fitted the band out with new outfits
and found them a gig at the Twist at the Top nightclub in Ilford – the
same name as their album. The guys stayed at the club as the resident
band for around five weeks before playing along the south coast and
in London. Their second single 'Twist at the Top' was quickly released,
with 'I Ain't Mad at You' as the B-side. The band now toured up north,
including Manchester, Newcastle, and their home city of Liverpool.

On 12 October 1962, Little Richard appeared at the Tower
Ballroom in New Brighton. Derry had ensured that he was present
and had a number of photographs taken of himself alongside his hero.
One well-known photo shows Derry, Joey Ankrah, Sugar Deen, and
the Beatles all together with the star that they all so admired. When
Little Richard took to the stage, Derry watched excitingly. However,
that excitement took over Derry who couldn't contain himself as his
idol burst into a number. Derry jumped up on the stage and began to
sing along with Little Richard, and even showed him how to bop. The
crowd loved it and went wild. The following day, Derry was invited
along to the Adelphi hotel, where Little Richard was staying. During
this meeting, Little Richard asked Derry to join him on his return to
America but Derry declined out of loyalty to his band.

Derry with Little Richard. (Photo by Les Chadwick and courtesy of Peter Kaye Photography)

Early in 1963, a third single was released by Fontana. The A-side 'The Boll Weavil Song' and the flip 'Bony Moronie' had both been taken from their album. Their records sold in a number of places, including Germany, but they were never able to break into the charts with them. The guys were looking in different directions as to where their future in music lay. Derry, who had a newly born son, returned home in search of work as the Seniors decided to call it a day.

Before we carry on, mention must be given to Howie Casey, who went on to play with Kingsize Taylor and the Dominoes in Hamburg. He also played with the Pawns, and the Krew, before becoming a session musician. Howie played on many hits and albums and backed many of the biggest stars around. He toured with Wings and played on their albums *Band on the Run*, *Wings at the Speed of Sound*, and *Back to the Egg*. His talents were spotted by the Who, leading to Howie touring with them and playing on the albums *Tommy*, and *Quadrophenia*.

By May 1963, Derry was once more fronting a band when he joined the Wallasey-based Pressmen. The band consisted of Ritchie Prescott (lead guitar), Bob Pears (bass), Phil Kenzie (sax), Dave Roberts (sax) and Tommy Bennett (drums). In their first few weeks together the band took part in a beat-band competition for Decca records. Whoever won would be given a recording contract. The Pressmen won but the contract was never given to them, with some believing that Decca refused it as Derry would not stand still behind a microphone. On 23 May the band recorded for Oriole records, along with others groups, at the Rialto Ballroom in Liverpool. The recordings were used to form the album *This is Merseybeat*. The Pressmen only had one song on the LP with Derry singing 'Hallelujah I Love Her So'.

The band went through a number of member changes over the next few months. They remained a very good and popular band who were doing well and had started playing further afield. On 17 September 1963, on the radio show called *Pop Go the Beatles*, the song 'Lucille' was dedicated to Derry Wilkie. They played a number of gigs at the Cavern up to the new year of '64. Then, and out of the blue, the band told Derry they were off to Germany to back Freddie Starr. Without any warning they just upped and went. Derry and the sax player Phil Kenzie were left with no band.

Derry went to London and sang with the Alexis Korner's Blues Incorporated, who he and the original Pressmen had played the same bill with at the Cavern Club in Liverpool on 28 September 1963. Derry and the Pressmen had also recorded a song called 'Can You Think Of Another?' that was not released, but can easily be found on the internet.

Back home in Liverpool, Derry and Phil decided to stick together and recruit new members for a band. Johnny 'Guitar' Byrne, from Rory Storm and the Hurricanes agreed to help Derry out for his first gig at the Iron Door Club. Johnny played guitar, Derry sang, and Phil played sax. Derek Bond joined them on bass, with Tommy Bennett on drums. They blew the club away with a real stormer of a set. Afterwards, Phil and Derry asked Derek if he would stay on as bass player, and he agreed. Ernie Hayes joined on lead guitar, with Norman Chapman on drums. Norman only played a few gigs before deciding that he did not want to play full time, so Mike Holmes replaced him. The band had become known as Derry Wilkie and the Others. They went down well on the local circuit, where they played most of the venues. They also became regular performers at the Kraal Club in New Brighton. During this period, Derry was also employed by Liverpool Art College as an artist's model. He also modelled for Arthur Dooley, with Arthur producing a number of busts of Derry for sale.

Derek Bond, bass player in the band, spoke about visiting Derry's home in Kent Gardens:

> One of my clearest recollections is of Derry taking his wife Eve's wedding ring to the pawnbrokers so that we could borrow enough money to hire a van to drive to gigs in Newcastle. Eve never seemed to mind on the few occasions that that happened. She always got her ring back after the band had been paid, but what an amazing lady to have even agreed in the first place.

The band found work in the north-east at places like Peter Stringfellow's Mojo Club in Sheffield, and Club a'GoGo in Newcastle, which was owned by the Animals' manager, Mike Jeffery. It was here that Eric Burden spotted Derry and the boys and convinced Mike Jeffery to sign them up to his agency. Mike sent the band to Germany in late 1964 to play the Star-Club circuit. While in Hamburg they stayed at the Hotel Pacific, where many of the Star-Club artists were put up. They were there at Christmas 1964 along with the Liverbirds, among others. The hotel restaurant had closed on Christmas Eve for a few days, so the musicians talked the hotel into letting them use the kitchen. They all chipped in, Derry included, and made a superb Christmas dinner that they all enjoyed together. While in Germany they played the same night as their former band members and Freddie Starr in Flensburg. They took up residence at the Star-Club in Colonge in early 1965 and stayed in Germany after their contract had ended. To get by they all played with any band that would pay them. In the end, Mike Jeffery paid for them all to return to Britain.

The guys then moved down to London. Billy Adamson replaced Mike Holmes on drums after Mike made it clear he had no intention of moving

Derry Wilkie on stage. (Courtesy of the Wilkie family collection)

to the capital. The guys gigged around London and the south. When they heard that the Pressmen were no longer using that name, they adopted it themselves and became, for Derry once more, Derry Wilkie and the Pressmen. They performed under this title when they supported the Alan

Price Set at the Marquee Club in November of 1965. Shortly after this, the band was approached by Screaming Lord Sutch, who had just lost most of his band members and was looking to replace them. Derry and the boys agreed to join him alongside his two remaining members, Noel Mcmanus and Ashton Tootell. The name of the Others/Presssmen was dropped, and they became Screaming Lord Sutch and the Savages.

They toured the UK and Germany, though it was a crazy show sometimes. For part of the act Derry would dress up as a woman and Lord Sutch would chase him around with a knife. On 4 February 1966, the Savages played alongside the Who, the MerseyBeats, and the Fortunes at the Astoria in Finsbury Park. This was the first of three dates that the four bands played together. The other two being 5 February at the Odeon in Southend-on-Sea, and the Liverpool Empire Theatre on the 6th. They played two shows at each venue over the three days. They also recorded the 'One Eyed Purple People Eater' as Lord Sutch and the Savages. When they were in Germany they appeared on a TV show called *Die Drehscheibe*. The former American boxer Freddie Mack approached the band about joining him for a stage show. The guys decided that it was what they wanted to do and broke away from Lord Sutch.

With the band in place they set about rehearsing before making their debut gig at the Ram Jam Club in Brixton. Derry was one of the singers in the band, who went by the name of Freddie Mack's This 'N' That. On 10 June 1966, under the name This 'N' That, they released a single on the Strike label called 'Get Down With It'. The song turns into the Rolling Stones 'I Can't Get No Satisfaction' halfway through. The B-side of the single went by the title of 'I Care About You'. It is uncertain if Derry is singing on the recording, though adverts in music papers from the time say that he is one of the singers on it. Derry left the band not long after the record came out, with the remainder of the original 'Others' leaving to pursue other projects.

By September 1966, Derry was back with Freddie Mack as part of his new set-up, playing under the name of the Freddie Mack Show. One of their first gigs together was at the Cavern Club in Liverpool on 10 September. They then played at a number of places around the UK, including the Whiskey-A-Go-Go club in Soho, London. On 21 December 1966, they became the house band at the newly opened Upper Cut Club on Woodgrange Road, East London. The club was owned by the former British Heavyweight boxer, Billy Walker. Here, Derry and the band opened up on the club's first night alongside the Who. The following night they billed with the Easybeats, the 23rd

Derry with a fan. (Courtesy of the Wilkie family collection)

with Dave Dee, Dozy, Beaky, Mick & Tich, and Christmas Eve with Eric Burden and the Animals. Boxing Day saw them playing an afternoon session alongside the Jimi Hendrix Experience and it was at this gig, while waiting to go on stage, that Jimi Hendrix is claimed to have written 'Purple Haze'. The 30th saw them with the Spencer Davis Group before they finished 1966 by playing at the club with Geno Washington and the Ram Jam Band.

They remained at the club until 12 February 1967, playing alongside bands of the calibre of the Small Faces, the Fourmost, the Move, plus another slot alongside Jimi Hendrix. They then performed around England and Scotland before Derry said his goodbyes and left the band before the summer of '67. Around this time, Mickie Most, the record producer, offered Derry a song to record that he said was a guaranteed top 10 hit. Derry turned it down as he wanted to do his own thing. The song was given to Dave Dee, Dozy, Beaky, Mick & Tich, and it charted as predicted.

By now, Derry's marriage to Eve was over and he ventured abroad. He spent some time in Paris, where he recruited a band of jazz musicians to accompany him to Italy. He toured around the country for a while with the band and he also appeared on TV there. To supply his income, Derry found a job dubbing over movies in English with that thick Scouse accent of his. His friend from Liverpool, Rita Martelli, recalled the night that she and Derry spotted each other in Rimini:

> I was on holiday in Italy. Myself and a few friends were sitting outside a local bar. We saw five black men walking up the street which was unusual at that time. As they came closer one of them started screaming and ran towards us. I also started screaming and ran to him as it was only Derry!! We could not believe it. He had a gig that night with the guys he was with who were American. I got in trouble with my then boyfriend, who became my husband, as I stood him up that night and went to see Derry perform at the L'Altro Mondo. Good times, he was a lovely man.

In October 1968, Derry bumped into Geno Washington and the Ram Jam Band, who he had played alongside at the Upper Cut Club in London. Geno invited Derry along to his gig at the Piper Club in Rome. It is unsure if their respective bands appeared on the same bill or if they guested with each other, though they definitely performed together a number of times before Geno and the guys moved on to Turin. Incidentally, the 1980 No. 1 single 'Geno' by Dexys Midnight Runners was written about Geno Washington.

Derry, along with his then-girlfriend, Eleanor, a lady from Ethiopia, and his Italian friend, Andro Cecovini, joined the cast of a show called *Orfeo 9*. This was the first rock opera in history to be staged. It was written, composed and directed by Tito Schipa Jr, and is a modern version of the myth of Orpheus and Eurydice. It played at the Teatro Sistina in Rome for a week from 23 January 1970. Derry was a soloist in the scene before the finale of the show. Orpheus finally finds Eurydice in Hell City but is so busy looking back at his past life that he cannot recognise her, and so we lose him forever. The girl comes on stage and a bluesman, in the guise of a storyteller, tells the story. Derry was the bluesman, singing the song 'Una Vecchia Favola' ('An Old Tale'), which, despite its title, was the only song in the show to be sung in English. Those with good eyesight may notice in the 1970 film the *Kremlin Letter* Derry dancing in a club for all of five seconds.

Sometime during 1970, Derry was at a house party in Rome the night before he was due to fly back to Britain. The house was raided by the police and Derry was found in possession of cannabis (one joint – he was partial to it at times) and was arrested. At his trial, he was found guilty and sentenced to three years in a Rome prison. When his mother found out, she went ballistic and campaigned for his

Derry performing as 'The Bluesman' in *Orfeo 9* at the Teatro Sistina in Rome. (Courtesy of Associazione Culturale Tito Schipa)

release. Via MPs, Grace petitioned the British Embassy to intervene. She also appeared on the TV programme *Weekend World* being interviewed about foreign justice and how Brits abroad are treated.

Derry's girlfriend Eleanor came to Liverpool and stayed with his mother Grace for six months. She worked as a waitress while she was here and also acted at the Shakespeare Theatre in Fraser Street. When Eleanor went back to Italy Grace went with her, stayed there for a few weeks, and visited her son every day. Visitors were allowed to take food and money in to give to the prisoners. Prison conditions were very poor and the inmates needed to be supported by family or friends to supplement their diet and provide toiletries. Sadly, the efforts to free Derry fell on deaf ears and he served all of his sentence.

By 1973 he was back home in Liverpool. Derry rarely spoke about his time in the Italian prison, though he did say that the possession charge had been a fit-up. As he was the only person charged from a party that had plenty of cannabis freely floating around, he may have had a good point. One thing he did pick up in Italy was the language, which he spoke very well. Derry met and began a relationship with Pat Lloyd and the couple had three children between them. Derry formed a number of bands in the 1970s and played around his home city. Two of his regular venues were at the Masonic in Berry Street and the Clock on the corner of Kingsley Road and Beaumont Street. He also performed an Elvis tribute show aboard the *Royal Iris*. Derry continued to work around Liverpool until 1981. He then decided to move back down to London.

In the summer of 1982, Derry married Donna Layfield in the capital and they settled in Chalk Farm, Camden. Here, Derry's skill of the Italian language came in handy with an elderly neighbour who would wait for Derry on the landing of their flats to engage him in rapid-fire Italian conversation. Derry used music to make a living once more, and played with a number of musicians and bands around London. One of the bands was called the Full Moon Boogie Band. In the mid-1980s he took his son, Wes, to watch Geno Washington playing a gig at the Bull and Gate in Kentish Town. Geno spotted Derry in the audience and asked him to sit in on a number or two, but Derry declined his invitation.

Derry's mother, Grace, along with other members of the family, was interviewed for the BBC documentary *Black Britain* in 1989. The first programme was broadcast on 7 January 1991. Grace appeared on it talking about her life in Liverpool and the hardships that people faced. She also recalled how she gave birth to Derry during a heavy air raid that demolished half of the street behind her home. The constant noise of exploding bombs and anti-aircraft guns was horrific and Derry had to be brought into the world by torchlight – you could say that Derry was born into the spotlight.

By the 1990s his marriage to Donna was over. Derry continued to do what he always had done: perform on stage. He became a regular at two pubs in Camden during the 1990s, playing at the Load Of Hay and the Sir Richard Steele. He played many of these gigs with Clive Robin Sarstedt and Tony Ashton. Derry would happily belt out classics such out 'Gimme Some Lovin', 'Twist and Shout', 'Whiter Shade Of Pale', and 'La Bamba'. He enjoyed living in Camden, where there were many ex-pats including a number of fellow Scousers. Beryl Marsden didn't live far away from here and they would sometimes bump into one another at the Washington pub in Belsize Park.

During the 1990s, Derry's partner, Mo, was diagnosed with cancer. For the next year, he nursed her until she sadly died. In the late 1990s Derry, himself, became ill. Tests discovered that he had a terminal illness. As it progressed, his mother decided that Derry should come home. On Derry's fifty-ninth birthday, she sent her youngest son, David, to London to persuade Derry to return to Liverpool. When David arrived in London, he found that Derry had been admitted hospital. When Derry saw David, he got himself out of bed and took the visit as an opportunity to show David around his old performing and drinking haunts. By the end of the visit and night out, David had persuaded Derry to return home to Liverpool. A few weeks later Derry made it home.

On his return to Liverpool, Derry initially lived in the family home but as his illness progressed and his mother became terminally ill too, he moved into sheltered accommodation in Linnets Lane. Here he had medical assistance on hand to help him with his illness. He was also now closer to many of his family members and oldest friends. Derry enjoyed spending days along Lodge Lane, where he would chat with friends old and new in the pubs and cafés. He was well liked and always the gentleman to people that he came into contact with.

One day he walked into a pub in Liverpool where a band was playing. They recognised him and asked him if he would sing a song with them. Derry agreed, and his performance brought the house down. During the last few months of 2001, his health became worse. Sadly, on 21 December of that year, Derry passed away. He was buried in Toxteth Park cemetery. When Derry was still alive his good friend Sugar Deen would ask family members about him and get them to pass on his regards. The family asked Sugar to speak at Derry's funeral service and he agreed and told a couple of stories. He ended by saying that they all should give Derry what any artist wants at the end: a round of applause. Sugar still visits his old buddy to say 'hello' whenever he is in Toxteth Cemetery.

Derry was the father to eleven children with Evangeline Welch, Ann Donnelly, Pat Lloyd, and Donna Layfield. He had one daughter named Star and eight sons: John (Jack), Edward, Wes, Ray, Desmond, Derry, Linton, David, Alexis, and Daniel. Sadly, Desmond passed away aged just a few weeks old. Derry was a very well-liked man who people speak very fondly of. As well as his friends in Liverpool, London, Germany, and Italy, he was also friends with Van Morrison, Geno Washington, Eric Burden, Edwin Starr, Alexis Korner, John Lennon, Paul McCartney, Ringo Starr, Cilla Black, Mick Jagger, Keith Richards, and Freddie Garrity among others. He left a lasting impression on those who knew him. People speak of the excitement of watching him perform, his friendliness, politeness, and his charming manners. They also mention his huge hands, which have been described as 'like shovels'. Derry's family and friends are extremely proud of him, as are fellow musicians and fans. Many remain in agreement that Derry should have been a big star. However, Derry was a star, a man who loved to perform and brought enjoyment to so many people. The legend of Derry Wilkie will never die away.

On 15 March 2003, Edwin Starr played a concert at the Philharmonic Hall in Liverpool, supported by Geno Washington. Edwin stopped during the performance to talk about Derry, telling the crowd how much he had enjoyed his company. Sadly, Edwin passed away just over two weeks later. On 26 October 2013, at St George's Hall, the inaugural Black Pioneer of Liverpool History award was posthumously given to Derry Wilkie.

Robin Sarstedt said of him:

Derry was a great showman who looked great all the time. A very good looking and polite man who came alive on a stage. He loved music and in my opinion he was more John Lennon than Paul McCartney. He also never lost that Scouse accent of his. I have great memories of drinking and jamming with Derry who is sadly missed.

Tony O'Keeffe, drummer with the Shakers, said:

In 1981 I was playing with a band called the Interns. During a gig at the Masonic pub in Berry Street in Liverpool, one of the guys spotted Derry Wilkie sitting at the bar and asked him would he give a song. Derry, dressed in an open shirt down to his naval, agreed and sang 'Midnight Hour' and 'Johnny B. Goode'. During one song Derry jumped onto a table, removed his shirt, and swung it around in the air. He was amazing and a brilliant showman. The pub erupted to him.

Howie Casey added, 'Derry was a lovely guy and a great performer. He is sadly missed.'

The author of this book would like to thank Derry's family for their help with his story. Also his friends and fellow musicians for providing such valuable input. I was rather stunned during the research to discover that so little information about Derry was available, especially on his later life. A lot of what had been written about him was incorrect and his family and friends wanted the story to be put straight here. Hopefully that has been corrected, and Derry has been given the credit that he deserves. Thank you, Derry Wilkie. Thank you for the music, the memories, and for being you – keep on shining.

Above: Derry Wilkie and the Pressmen performing at the Majestic Ballroom in Birkenhead.

Left: Derry Wilkie. (Courtesy of David Roberts)

3

The Liverbirds

Mary McGlory was born on 2 February 1946 in Burlington Street, Vauxhall, to Joseph McGlory and Margaret Dunn. Joseph was a merchant seaman when he met Margaret, who was then working as a conductress on the trams. Joseph later went to work at the Clarence Dock power station and Margaret was a school cleaner. Mary came from a strong Catholic family and had desires of becoming a nun.

One night in early 1962, Mary, her friend Margaret Cecchini, and two cousins, Veronica Dunne and Rita Wallace, went along to the Cavern to see the Beatles perform. Afterwards, they all agreed it would be a great idea to form an all-girl band. Mary's cousin Veronica said, 'our John can play a bit of guitar so he can teach us.' Within a couple of weeks they had been to Hessy's and bought three guitars and a set of drums – all on HP of course. They decided to call themselves the Squaws, bought outfits, and even had photographs taken. They then began taking their guitars with them when they went to the Cavern. This meant that they could just walk straight in – no waiting, no paying – just by saying they were a girl group. These forward-thinking girls also went along to the *Mersey Beat* office to talk to Bill Harry, who wrote a small article about them. Strangely enough, the article gave their name as the Bikinis, though this had never been their name. A later copy of the *Mersey Beat* paper showed a photograph of the girls and announced that they had changed their name from the Bikinis to the Squaws.

Bob Wooler kept asking when they would play at the Cavern. They decided that maybe it was about time they finally had a practice; after all, they couldn't play a note between them. They all sat together around cousin John and, what a shock, these guitars were a lot harder to play than they thought; in fact, they were hopeless. They realised that they would have to give up and decided to stay at home for a few weeks until everybody had forgotten about their band. About two weeks later there was a knock at Mary's front door and when she went to open it she was greeted by two girls called Valerie Gell and Sylvia Saunders. They told Mary they had heard that the band had split-up, and that they wanted to start a group and were looking for a bass and a rhythm player. Mary had been marked down to play rhythm in the Squaws, with her cousin Rita on bass. Val suggested that Rita and Mary came to her house a few days later to talk about a band.

Val lived with her parents in a house in Seaforth Road. When Mary and Rita arrived they said that they were interested in joining, Rita even said that one of the women she worked with in the cleaners on Great Homer Street had come up with a great name for a girl group – the Liverbirds. Val had her guitar and amp and she started playing some instrumentals, which was when Mary and Rita realised that she was really good. Sylvia was already having drumming lessons, so these two were musical. When Mary and Rita left they both decided they were never going back there again, as Val and Sylvia would laugh their heads off at them for being unable to play. A few weeks later, Sylvia and Val were back knocking at Mary's house. Val said, 'I suppose you can't play but at least you have the guitars and I can teach you.' Rita decided that she wanted out, but Mary had another cousin called Sheila McGlory who could play a bit of rhythm guitar. Mary had been supposed to play rhythm but Val said, 'no problem Mary, you can play bass, I will teach you'. And, with that, the Liverbirds were formed.

Valerie Gell was born on 14 August 1945 in Crosby. She was the daughter of Thomas Gell and Joyce McParlin, who had married in Durham after meeting in the army. Tom was a docker, while Joyce worked in an office. Sylvia Saunders was born on 31 October 1946 in Litherland. Her parents were Christopher Saunders and Gertrude Hignett. Christopher had gone to sea with the merchant navy and worked as a crane driver on the docks. He once played football against a Brazilian team (using jackets as goalposts) at the Maraccana stadium in Rio. Gertrude worked in a flour mill, as a petrol pump attendant, and in a fish and chip shop. She was also the first person to drive an electric milk float around the Litherland area. Gertrude later worked for the post office in Seaforth, where one of her co-workers was Keith (Sam) Hardie, who would later join the Dominoes.

Now that the four of them were together they decided to start serious practising. By now Mary was starting to play a few notes on the bass. They would meet every day after work to rehearse. Val worked in Owen Owens, while the other three had office jobs. The only place that they could play was in their own homes. So, and to be fair on the neighbours, they chose to take turns. One week in Sylvia's in Litherland, one week in Sheila's in Gilmoss, and one week in Mary's house in Ternhall Road in Fazakerley. Val's house was too small to use. They decided to practice from Monday to Friday every week, ensuring that they kept Saturday's free so they had time to go to clubs and watch other groups play. Sheila and Mary would go to have guitar lessons in a house in Rodney Street every Sunday, while Sylvia had her drum tuition. As it turned out, they had no need to worry about the neighbours complaining about the noise – they thought it was great. They even had to open the windows so that the children in the street could sit on the wall outside cheering. For the first few weeks they probably sounded awful, but those outside did not appear to mind.

Mary got the other girls to do what she had done with the Squaws: go to the Cavern with their guitars and get in for nothing. They would tell Bob Wooler that they were the Liverbirds and promised him they would play the club. One night in the Cavern, Bob introduced the girls to John Lennon and Paul McCarthy in the dressing room. He told them 'this will be our first all-female group' and John Lennon said, 'what girls with guitars, that will never work out'. The girls remain convinced that John said that to make them more determined.

Mary recalled a day that they were all practising in her house when there was a knock at the door. Standing there were two men from Cranes music shop. Mary and Sheila had bought their amps from Cranes, but Mary had failed to keep up her payments and so the men took her amp away. Val said, 'never mind Mary,' and plugged her bass into her amp. After they had been practising for some months they thought it was about time to try playing a gig. Father Bradley, a very nice young priest from Mary's parish, said that they could play for the old age pensioners who met once a week in the hall of her former school, St Philomena's, in Sparrowhall Road. And that became their first booking!

They girls had originally decided to play as an instrumental band, but after performing their first few public gigs they came to the conclusion that a singer was needed. However, instrumental or not, the band was getting a lot of bookings from agencies. They even found themselves appearing on TV for the Granada show *Scene at Six-thirty*. They bought themselves new outfits for the show – brown polo tops with black skiing trousers – and they thought they looked great. The driver who took them to Manchester went on a wild detour and it took them hours to get there. They had travelled in their new outfits, and the first question they were asked as they walked into the studio was 'Would you like to get changed first?' So much for great outfits. They were also informed that there was no time to rehearse as they would be going on pretty soon. The girls played their song; it was one where Sylvia would stand up at the end and scream as the band thought that it made it a bit more interesting. However, because they had not had time to rehearse, the people in the studio had no idea that the scream was coming so they thought that there was something wrong and all ran towards Sylvia. This was all seen by the people watching on their TV sets.

The band members opted to give up their day jobs and turn professional. They also ditched their TV outfits and asked Val's cousin Ted to make them new ones as he was a tailor. They chose bright-red thick cord trousers and vests. Ted was delayed in getting them finished, so the girls had no time to try them on before travelling to a booking in Chester. In Mary's own words, 'my god we looked terrible – like four fat Father Christmas's, we couldn't stop laughing.'

They now decided it was time for them to start looking for a singer. An advert was placed in the *Liverpool Echo* and the response was pretty big. After auditions, they chose Irene Greene to front them. Now with a singer, they were able to play songs such as 'Boys' or 'Da Doo Ron Ron'. Once again they went into a rigid set of practice sessions. In the meantime, Ted got to work on more outfits: dark-blue glittery skirts with dark blouses and braces. The rehearsals paid off and the girls began gigging around the local area. They impressed and went down well with the audiences who witnessed them on stage.

One night after playing at a very popular club in Manchester with Dave Berry and a few other groups, one of the bands, who shall remain nameless, asked, 'why don't you come and pay us a visit for a few days and we will show you Manchester'. The whole group lived together in a house and the girls could stay with them. A few days later, Val, Sylvia, and Mary jumped on a train and off they went. Well, it turned out to be their first confrontation with 'groupies'. Girls were coming and going all day at the house. The Liverbirds were shocked and Mary, being a good Catholic girl, was disgusted. That was it, the next morning they were on the train back home. Even when she began to play music in a band, Mary still thought she would only be doing it for a couple of years before dedicating herself to her faith and becoming a nun.

They caught the eye of a number of agencies, who began to offer them work. The bookings were coming in good and saw them doing lots of one-week to ten-day tours between Scotland and southern

England. It was on one of these tours that they played with the Rolling Stones when they were just beginning to be well known. They were really interested in the Liverbirds and they would all have a good laugh in the dressing room. When Mary was on stage one night, one of her bass strings broke. That was the first time that this had happened to her and she did not know what to do. Mary became upset and started crying, but within seconds Bill Wyman came on stage to give her his bass and took hers away to replace the string. A while later, the girls were on their way back to Liverpool after doing a booking somewhere around London. They stopped at one of the service stations that go from one side of the motorway to the other like a bridge. When they arrived at the café, the Stones were just leaving; they were on their way back to London after playing somewhere in the north. Brian Jones saw them coming and shouted the others back, saying 'come back, here are the Liverbirds'. Then they all then sat down and had coffee together.

The next thing that they needed to do was to find themselves a roadie. Val's dad knew somebody who used to work with him on the docks called Bob, who had bought himself a van and started driving groups around. He agreed to become their roadie, but because he had one or two other groups to look after he informed them that he may not be able to drive them all of the time. This was all fine as Sylvia's brother-in-law – another Bob – who had been helping them out with the driving, said that he would take over when 'Bob-the-roadie' could not drive them.

One night after playing at the Cavern, the girls had their guitars stolen out of the van. They were horrified as they were still struggling to pay them off and there was no way that they could afford new ones. Mary had an auntie who was a very well-known barrow woman in the city centre. Her mother told her to go and see her Aunt Crissie, as she may be able to help. Mary visited her aunt, who two days later informed Mary that the guitars were at her house and to come and pick them up. She never explained to them how she managed to get them back, but the girls were just thankful to have them again.

The tours were great for the band, who found themselves playing alongside the likes of the Rockin' Berries and the Rolling Stones. It was a wonderful thrill, experience, and stage to highlight their talents. One night when they were playing at the a'GoGo in Newcastle, Irene told them that she wanted to leave the band to do her own thing, but agreed that she would stay until they found a replacement. Somebody at the club said one of the girls working there could sing. Her name was Heather and she sang for the girls who took her back with them to Liverpool the next day. It was a strange evening at the club in Newcastle with so much happening. One of the groups had not turned up and the owner asked the girls to play an extra set. Sylvia's brother-in-law went to deal with him about how much extra he would be paying them. He told the owner that he should be paying them double as they were playing twice, but he protested saying, 'They are already getting paid a lot.' In the end he agreed and paid the extra fee in cash. When the girls saw how much it was they were stunned as it was a lot more than they had been led to believe that their fee actually was. Basically, they had been lied to about what club owners were paying to book them and some people were making money by deceiving them. This upset the band and left them feeling as if they were being used and cheated by agencies as they were girls. And that is what was happening. It was blatant discrimination against an all-female group. You have to remember that they were, at this time, still young girls, aged between sixteen and seventeen. The treatment they received had left them hurt and deflated. They were beginning to doubt if the music industry was for them. That night in Newcastle was also the night they heard the announcement over the microphone that President Kennedy had been shot.

Back home in Liverpool they practised with Heather and started looking for agents that would not cheat them. Their parents were beginning to worry if this was the right business for young girls. Poor Heather was really homesick and they knew it would not last with her. The band went on a short tour in Crewe with a new up-and-coming band called the Kinks. They really got along well together and the girls were able to talk to the lads about their problems. Sheila was also not fitting in too well as she was just too shy. Ray Davis said, 'There is a girl here tonight from Liverpool, she just told me that she can play guitar and sing.' He then introduced them to Pamela Birch, who agreed to join the band. Ray Davis said, 'When you feel you are ready, come down to London and meet our manager.' Heather went back home, and Sheila returned to her job.

Pam had been born on 9 August 1944 in the Kirkdale area of the city. Her parents were George Birch and Alma Percy, who had both met in the army. The family later went to live in Speke when George found work at the Ford factory there. Alma was a head cook in a school canteen. After leaving school, Pam found work with a law firm in Liverpool city centre. She also played and sang in a duo alongside her sister Diane. They proved to be rather good and won a number of talent competitions across Merseyside.

The Liverbirds. (Courtesy of The Liverbirds Collection)

Once more the band went into a period of intense rehearsals. They soon realised that Pam was going to change things in the group as regards the way that they dressed and played. She talked Val into starting to sing and with their two voices together allowed the band to start playing things like Chuck Berry, Bo Diddly and Muddy Waters. Their voices mixed well and would go together on the rhythm and blues songs that they were beginning to learn after playing alongside the Rolling Stones. The Stones had become a big influence on the band, who wanted to sound more like them than anyone else.

On one of the girl's visits to Bill Harry at the *Mersey Beat* office, he informed them that the official agent of the Star-Club, a man named Henry Henroid, was coming to Liverpool to audition groups for the club. That was just about the dream of every group at the time. The auditions were taking place on Sunday at the Rialto. The Liverbirds auditioned and Henry said straight away that he wanted them as soon as possible. There was just one problem: Sylvia was not eighteen yet so would have to get court permission, which could take a while. Henry said he would get in touch with the owner of the club, Manfred Weissleder, to see what he could do. Henry then asked them if they would like to come with him to meet a group from Hamburg called the Rattles who were playing at the Cavern that night. Of course, the girls agreed, and he took them to a small hotel on Mount Pleasant called the Mycroft where a lot of the groups stayed when they were playing at the club. The girls became very friendly with the landlady and often went there for a cup of tea when they were feeling down. After meeting the Rattles, Henry gave them a lift in their van to watch them play.

Time was something that the girls did not have on their side. Their parents were getting really worried about the uncertainty over what was happening with regard to the Star-Club. The Liverbirds realised that it was time to try to get themselves a manager, and, just like that, they decided to go down to London and try to meet Brian Epstein. They bought one-way train tickets to London as they could not afford returns, and off they went. The girls did not even have anywhere to stay. They chose to sit in a coffee bar until they were thrown out and then sleep in a park before making their way to Brian's office the next day. Just how crazy were these girls, who would go to any lengths to get what they needed? The next part of the evening seems unbelievable, but it really happened. They were all sitting in a coffee bar at Piccadilly Circus around 11 p.m. when Pam looked out of the window and said, 'there's Brian Epstein'. With that, the four of them ran out and started chasing after him. Brian saw four young girls running towards him and must have thought that they were mad Beatles fans, so he ran down into Piccadilly tube station. The girls caught up with him and quickly told him who they were and what they wanted. He gave them his card and told them to come to his office the next morning. They did not tell him, of course, that they had nowhere to sleep, and went off to find a park. Lord knows what they must have looked like when they arrived at his office the next day. He was very nice and understanding and said that he would arrange for them to play somewhere close to London as soon as possible and come along to watch. When the girls informed Brian they had no train tickets back to Liverpool, he called his secretary and asked her to buy them the tickets.

True to his word, Brian found the girls a gig in London the following Sunday, and they got their roadie to drive them there. When they arrived at the club a man came over and introduced himself, informing them that Brian had sent him as he had not been able to come himself. After the band had performed, he told them he thought they were very good and that Mr Epstein would be in touch. The girls were all disappointed that Brian had not come himself and came to the conclusion that maybe he wasn't really interested in them.

The Liverbirds. (Courtesy of The Liverbirds Collection)

Back in Liverpool, the band remembered what the Kinks has said to them. Pam phoned Ray as he had given her his number, and it was arranged for them to come to London. Larry Page paid their train fare and even booked them into a hotel. Ray and Dave Davies met the girls in London and took them to their hotel. They then asked them to come along to the studio with them as they were recording that day. They also told them to bring their guitars with them in case there was a chance for them to play a song for the Kinks' manager, Larry. On arrival at the studio, the Kinks were informed by their roadie that their guitars had been stolen from the van. Pam, Mary and Val stood there holding their guitars, which they had brought along as asked, so the Kinks asked if they could play them during the session and the girls agreed. They then sat watching as 'You Really Got Me' was recorded. The song was also recorded on another day, so the girls have no idea if it is their guitars or not that are being played on the hit record. Even though Dave Davies says he cannot recall this ever happening, his brother Ray, who Mary met up with in Hamburg in around 2005, could remember it when he chatted with her.

Another band was waiting to use the studio after the Kinks finished, but they were persuaded to allow the Liverbirds to play one song for Larry; the girls chose 'Reelin and Rockin'. Mr Page was impressed as the girls performed. Ray Davies had joined in with the band on guitar, while the Rolling Stones' roadie, Ian Stewart, who had been in the studio at the time, played piano. The engineers recorded the song as they played and the band members of the Liverbirds still have that demo track in their possession.

Shortly afterwards, Henry got back in touch and said Manfred had decided to book us into the Aaland hotel in Bloomsbury and start fighting to get Sylvia's court permission. This was a hotel where lots of groups stayed at the time. Here, they met a girl named Hannah, who turned out to be the hotel groupie. Hannah used to keep them entertained in the evenings as they had no money to go out, telling them stories about her experience with some of the groups. The girls were stunned and had never heard stories such as these and they certainly had never even dreamt that they could happen.

The court work permit for Sylvia was taking longer than expected, and the girls were left sitting around twitching their thumbs. To play at the Star-Club in Hamburg was a dream to them and they were longing to go over and get started there. They also had to contend with worried parents, who wondered why their young daughters were still in a hotel in London. We can only guess what their worries were about the girls going over to Hamburg. Their parents, who had been sending them money to live off, were by now phoning and telling them to come home. Henry was footing the bill for their rooms at the hotel but all other expenses had to be met by the band themselves and funds were getting to a seriously low level. The girls had to eat, and could not keep asking for help. They quickly needed to make some money.

Jimmy Saville, who had a room at the hotel, had the idea of getting a reporter from the newspaper the *Sunday People* to pay the girls to do an article about the band. A reporter came the next day with a photographer. He explained that he was willing to pay them £100 for an interview and photographs. The band agreed as this was a huge amount of money for that time, which would easily get them through the next few weeks and keep their parents happy for a while. The interview was taken and the photo session commenced outside on the hotel steps with shouts of 'Smile! Don't smile! Look happy! Sad! Jump up in the air! Sit down' and on and on and on. Afterwards, the girls were happy for they had earned a decent fee and bagged themselves some publicity. They were very pleased with their day's work indeed. However, their joy fell apart when they saw the Sunday newspaper. There, splashed across the front page for all to see, was a photograph of them looking really downhearted under a headline that said something along the lines of 'Don't let this happen to your daughters'. Well, that was it, their parents were on the phone telling them to get home right away. They had been well and truly stitched-up. Once more, it was a lesson learned for the band towards the trust they should be wary of placing in others. Fortunately, Henry had realised that he needed someone famous to help him with the case and had been able to get his friend, Mickie Most, to go to court with him and swear that Sylvia would be taken care of in Hamburg. That did the trick, and the next day Henry and Mickie took them to the station and put them on the train for their journey to Germany.

During their stay in London, the girls had impressed the Kinks' manager Larry Page so much at the recording studio that he had offered to manage them. Brian Epstein had also sought out a meeting with the band during this time and he made his intentions clear that he would like them to sign a managerial contract with him. The girls, however, only had eyes for the Star-Club and Hamburg at this time. Plus, they could decide on these two offers once they returned back to the UK.

The Liverbirds arrived in Hamburg on 28 May 1964, taking a taxi from the train station to the Star-Club. Mary, who was a devout Catholic, recalled their arrival:

> The cab pulled up in the street next to the Kaiserkeller club and the first thing that I saw was the wonderful St Joseph church. It was so beautiful and made me feel at ease. Then we turned the corner into the Grosse Freiheit and were greeted by the many strip joints and bars. What a contrast.

The girls barely had time to bring in their gear before they were introduced to the Star-Club owner, Manfred Weissleder, who informed them that they would be playing that same evening. The club had billed them as '*Die weiblichen* Beatles' (the female Beatles). The band took to the famous stage and opened up with 'Money'. They decided that during the lead's break the three girls up front would turn and wiggle their bums at the audience, as they did the crowd cheered and threw money onto the stage. The girls were excited, yet nervous, for they had heard of how tough it could be for new bands to please the barmaids at the club. Above the bar hung lamps that the barmaids would swing whenever they liked the sound of a new band. Being an all-girl band the Liverbirds fretted even more and kept glancing towards the bar. Sure enough, the lamps began to swing and the girls were delighted. Manfred loved them as well and could clearly see their potential.

The girls take a break from practice. Spot the Star-Club bag and record player. (Courtesy of The Liverbirds Collection)

A few days later he sent them to play in Berlin at a huge concert that was being topped by Chuck Berry. Before any band was allowed on stage, they were first warned not to perform any Chuck Berry numbers. The Liverbirds' set consisted of a number of Chuck's songs and they were not in any mood to change it all at the last minute. So, on to the stage they went, with Val grabbing the microphone and announcing that they were going to play 'Roll Over Beethoven'. Chuck's manager ran onto the stage waving his arms and tried to stop the band from playing. As he did, Val pushed him and told him to 'f*ck off'. On their arrival back in Hamburg, they were summoned to Manfred's office. They feared that they were in trouble and expected Manfred to explode at them, but nothing could be further from the truth. In fact, Chuck Berry's manager was also impressed with the band, even though they had shoved and insulted him, and he wanted to take them to America. Manfred told the girls that he would leave the decision up to them, but added 'he will probably take you to Las Vegas, and there you will have to play topless'. Of course, that was Manfred's way of trying to put the girls off, and why not? They could crowd out his club whenever they played. In fact, it was more than full every night, with the queues going right down the Grosse Freiheit.

Their original contract had been for four weeks. During this time the group had impressed both audience and club owner. The girls relied on their abilities to perform instead of their feminine charms, as was the case with so many female performers. Their masculine outfits, right down to the winkle pickers, added to their rocking sound and stage routines – it all made them stand out. You have to credit them for doing it their own way. They were being noticed, with a fan base already starting to form for them at the Star-Club, and Manfred wanted them. A meeting was called and a rolling contract at the club was offered. This also included a recording deal with the Star-Club record label and it made Manfred their manager. The girls signed without hesitation. They loved the Star-Club, Hamburg, and Germany. It was a fantastic deal for them and the offers made by Larry Page and Brian Epstein were no longer of any interest to them, though the girls remained thankful to both for wanting to manage their careers. The signing of Manfred's contract also changed the future for the girls. As you will see, Germany became much more than just a workplace for them.

The band continued to play at the Star-Club, where they remained a crowd favourite. Studio work began and in December 1964 they released their first single with their version of the Berry Gordy and Smokey Robinson song 'Shop Around'. For the B-side they recorded 'It's Got To Be You', which had been composed by their very own Pam Birch. The year 1965 started with the release of their first album *Star-Club Show 4*.

In April of that same year the band released their second single, with a cover of the Bo Diddley song *Diddley Daddy*. The B-side once again consisted of a song penned by Pam Birch in the shape of 'Leave All Your Loves in the Past'. The single made it into the German top 40 singles chart and rose to No. 5. This was enough to bring the band to the attention of a wider German audience. It also brought interest from a number of TV and magazine companies who were keen on covering the group. An article about the Liverbirds was published in the hugely followed German teen magazine *Bravo*, while appearances followed for the band on the popular music TV programme *Beat Club*. They also toured Europe, playing in Germany, Austria, Switzerland, Holland, Denmark and Norway. Their popularity was huge with the Germans, who were taking to the band to their hearts.

In June 1965, the band released their third single, 'Peanut Butter'. The song was a version of the 1961 Marathons single and had been recorded on 13 April for the Star-Club label. It became one of their most popular tracks. The B-side was the rather wonderful 'Why Do You Hang Around Me', which was once again a Pam Birch original. On 25 September 1965, the girls were given a three-song slot on the *Beat Club* TV show, where they sang 'Peanut Butter', 'Why Do You Hang Around Me' and 'Diddley Daddy'. You can see their performance on the show by searching

Liverbirds Sylvia and Mary taking a break. (Courtesy of The Liverbirds Collection)

YouTube. The exposure from TV and music magazines was bringing the band to a wider German audience, which resulted in a number of work offers. In February 1966 the Rattles starred in the first German beat film – *Hurra, Die Rattles Kommen*. The Liverbirds also appeared in the film, performing two of the songs from their forthcoming second album: 'Peanut Butter' and 'Around and Around'.

Their fourth single 'Loop de Loop' a Joe Dong and Teddy Vann composition, was released in May 1966. No Pam Birch written number was included on the B-side, as had become the norm. Instead, the band recorded 'Bo Diddley Is a Lover' for the flip side. The single sadly never made the German charts and their upcoming album *More Of*, although selling, never made the dent to the charts that it needed to.

So much had changed for the Liverbirds since they had first arrived in Hamburg, and by 1967 life-changing events were starting to unfold. Val had married her boyfriend Stephan Hausner, with their wedding taking place in the summer of 1966 at Crosby registry office in Liverpool. Sylvia was Val's maid of honour. Sylvia had been dating John Wiggins, the keyboard player from the Bobby Patrick Big Six band, sometimes known as the Big Six. The band had been Star-Club regulars, and Sylvia and John had met and fallen in love. Plans were made for a wedding and starting a home together in Hamburg. Sylvia and John were married in August 1967 at the British Consulate in Hamburg. Their reception was attended by all the bands who were playing at the Star-Club, and it lasted all day and into the next morning.

Yamaha contacted the band, offering them a tour of Japan at the beginning of 1968 but Sylvia and Val decided that it was not for them.

Sylvia snaps the other three in the hotel Pacific. Spot those Star-Club tops. (Courtesy of The Liverbirds Collection)

Reluctant to put their married lives on hold for a tour, they agreed that replacement members should be found so that the tour could go ahead. Mary and Pam found two German girls – Christiane Shultz on guitar and Renate Wassemeyer (known as Dixie) on drums – to join them for the forthcoming tour. The Japanese loved the band and it was a great experience. However, for Pam and Mary it was not the same without Val and Sylvia. At the end of the Japanese tour they both decided to quit. The Liverbirds were no more. The girls were aged between twenty-two and twenty-three at the conclusion of the band. Still rather young, when you consider how much they had achieved. Mary went on to marry Frank Dostal in Hamburg. Frank had been the singer with the German band the Rattles and became a successful songwriter. He co-wrote, among others, the 1977 hit 'Yes Sir, I Can Boogie'. Pam never married. Sadly, she passed away on 27 October 2009. Pam's sister, Dyan, went on to sing with 'Arrival', with whom she sang main vocals on the 1970 hit 'Friends'. She later joined another successful band, Kokomo.

Liverpool should be proud to have the Liverbirds as its daughters. Sadly, the UK never appeared to take them seriously, which is to the British music industry's absolute shame for ignoring these talented Scouse girls. However, the Kinks and the Rolling Stones knew that this band was rather special and unique. The UK's loss was Germany's gain, with the Germans welcoming a band that thrilled and entertained them. The Liverbirds loved Germany and its people so much that they remained there to work and set-up home. In 2010, Ace Records released the album *From Merseyside to Hamburg*, featuring twenty-nine songs that were recorded by the Liverbirds. The album's release in Britain made it the first official recording made by the band to be brought out there – it had only taken the Brits around forty-five years to catch on. Mary, Val, and Sylvia were very proud of this album, their only regret being that Pam was not still alive to see it happen.

So, just how important where the Liverbirds in musical history and development? The answer is 'groundbreaking'. They are described as the 'first all-female rock band'. That statement is probably true, and they were perhaps the first female rock band to play and record professionally. Goldie and the Gingerbreads have also been given that title, though their first band was not all female. Comparing the two bands as to who did what first would be futile, as they were both pioneer bands who broke the mould for women in the music industry. Both bands also appeared on the same bill on a number of occasions. The Liverbirds gave a voice to women within a male-dominated industry and provided inspiration for many girls to take up music, compete with, and show the guys that they could do it just as well. You have to admire the chances that these girls took in their early days as they sought to and break through into industry set out for men. Their determination is admirable, and it is easy to see why they found the success that they did.

The four ladies have all stayed close throughout the years and have attended a number of reunions and special events. The last time that they appeared together as a band was in 2000. During my research for this book I have worked closely with Mary, Sylvia, and Val, and found them warming and at times very funny people. They wanted me to express the importance, alongside their own gratitude, towards two people: Henry Henroid, their booking agent and close friend, who the girls describe as a wonderful man; and Manfred Weissleder, their manager, who believed in them as they bloomed. The band knew when they signed for him that he was the one for them. In their own words: 'Manfred was our one and only manager and he always will be. We never needed, nor wanted to be managed by anyone else. We thank him for everything.'

Sadly, as this book was being written, Val passed away on 11 December 2016 in Lübeck, Germany. Val was a talented guitarist and a great singer with a distinctive voice. She was a wonderful person who will be missed by all who knew her. Sylvia had this to say about her old friend: '2016 was the year that they took so many musical greats. It is little surprise that they wanted Val to be with them.'

The Liverbirds pose on motor bikes. (Courtesy of The Liverbirds Collection)

4

Johnny 'Guitar' Byrne

John Byrne was born on 4 December 1939 in Liverpool to Michael Patrick Byrne and Elsie Ford. Michael was a Seaman who was born on 22 October 1908. Elsie had been born on 10 July 1905 in Liverpool. She spent her early years living at No. 2 Belfast Road in the Old Swan area of the city, where he lived with her sister and four brothers. Elsie's parents – Elizabeth (née Cowan) and Henry, a coal dealer – had married in 1898 and had moved to the Old Swan area from Everton. Elsie had married Michael in the city in 1932. A year later, Michael's work had taken him and Elsie to London, where their first two children, Patrick and Norma, were born. The family returned to Liverpool when Michael's employers decided to relocate him in that city. They found and settled into a house at No. 37 Oakhill Park, which is just off Broad Green Road. Here, both John and his brother Paul were born. John was educated at St Oswald's school and was part of the church of the same name.

Around the age of eleven, he was struck down with rheumatic fever. He survived and spent six months convalescing in a hospital up in Southport. He returned home and became a member of the local boys' club on Derby Lane. He also took dance lessons at Martin's dance school, situated next door to the boys' club. Both buildings remain in use for the same purpose today, though the boys' club is now a youth club. John was a lover of horror and an avid collector of anything to do with the subject.

John's interests were soon to change from horror, and all because of his elder brother. Pat would bring home the 78 rpm records and John would listen, fascinated, to the likes of Gerry Mulligan, Stan Kenton, and Johnny Dankworth. He first heard Elvis Presley on one of Paul's 78s and it knocked him out. However, the song that changed everything for him was 'Rock Island Line' by Lonnie Donegan. That is the song that made him want to play music, and when he saw Lonnie performing on TV he thought to himself 'I could do that', but first he needed a guitar. An advert in a newspaper offered a Spanish guitar for £8. John sent away for one and when it arrived he thought 'what an ugly colour'. When it arrived he was stunned. The guitar had no scratch-board, but John soon fixed that with a bit of imaginative DIY. When John tried to play the guitar he realised, as we all do, that he was going to need help to learn. He knew a lad who lived close to him named Allen Thompson, who played with a band called the Rhythm Quartet. John asked him if he would show him how to play and Allen agreed. Over the next couple of months, Allen taught John to play chords and a number of tunes. John was so dedicated to learning that he would spend hours in his bedroom practising the chords that he had learned. John soon mastered a few chords and songs, but he knew that the only way he would get better was by performing, but who could he team up with?

On 24 March 1956, John was returning to his home by bus. He was sat playing his guitar as the bus trundled on. A tall blond lad came over to him and said, 'Hi'. His name was Alan Caldwell, and he liked how John played the guitar. John offered to let Alan play it, but he told him that he did not know how to. As the two lads continued to chat they discovered that they both lived very close to one another. John told Alan that he would teach him to play the guitar, and that was the start of a firm friendship. The two of them got to work and Alan soon picked up a few chords. In November 1956, they both went along to watch a Lonnie Donegan concert at the Liverpool Empire theatre. So excited were they by the show that they sat up talking throughout the night about forming a band. First, however, they needed to recruit a few members. With this done, they rehearsed enough to play a simple set that included 'Maggie May', 'Rock Island Line', and 'Don't You Rock Me Daddy-O'. They were now ready and eager to perform in front of an audience. Under the name of Alan Caldwell's Skiffle Group they began to find themselves gigs, with most of them being around the pubs and halls of the Old Swan area where they lived.

Bill Haley and the Comets came to Liverpool in February 1957 to play at the Odeon Cinema. John was unable to get himself a ticket for the show and was distraught. Alan, even though he had a ticket, posed as a workman alongside John to gain access to the building.

The Texans. (Courtesy of Margaret Byrne)

Once inside, they hid until the band began to play. John could not take his eyes off the electric guitars, and decided there and then that he was going to get one. John had soon convinced his father to sign the hire-purchase document that resulted in a semi-acoustic Aristone guitar falling into John's hands.

On 24 May 1957, the band played at the Cavern Club alongside the Muskrat Jazz Band and the Gin Mill Skiffle Group. It was no amazing gig, but the lads did OK. However, the importance of this event in musical history should not be allowed to just pass us by. John and Alan became the first performers from the later Mersey sound era to play the Cavern Club. Their gig set the wheels in motion for the music and association that would turn the Cavern into one of the most important venues in the world. John provided us with another first when he and a friend, Paul Murphy, decided to record a song at the Percy Phillips recording studio in Kensington on 22 June 1957. They played Little Richard's 'She's Got It', and a song called 'Butterfly'. They were recorded and transferred onto a disc, thus making John and Paul the first Merseybeat people to record on a disc.

A Mrs Thompson owned a very big, old house called Balgownie in Oakhill Park, near to John's house. She allowed the band to practise there in the basement. The group changed their name to Al Caldwell's Texans and began to enter a number of talent competitions. When the Jim Dale Skiffle contest came to the Empire theatre, they entered and made it all the way through to the final. They finished runners-up to a group named Darktown – a great achievement and fantastic experience for them. The guys wanted to play rock and roll, but venue owners still wanted skiffle music. John and Alan hit upon the idea of their own club and went to talk to Mrs Thompson. With her agreement (she was way ahead of her time) they opened a club in the house basement called the Morgue. The Texans, Quarrymen, and Bluegenes all played here. A protesting neighbour managed to have the club shut down after six weeks. It was a great effort by John and Alan, and the number of punters they brought in had proved that such a venue was indeed popular.

John took a number of jobs, but his lack of interest in them led to him constantly being sacked. His interest was music, and he needed an income to obtain better equipment. He took a job with a firm called Platt's at the Cotton Exchange. Of course, he hated it, but he needed the money and stuck with it. He was employed as an invoice clerk, who worked out the cotton weights for ships.

The People's National Talent competition at Butlins Pwllheli was a contest that took their interest. John and Alan easily won their heats, before cruising to victory in the final when performing 'Rock Island Line' and 'John Henry'. A prize of £3 and a free holiday was enough to send them home feeling like superstars. It also gave them an idea of where they wanted to go with the band, whose members had changed on a regular basis. It was time to become more serious and by April 1959 it was beginning to take shape, when another Old Swan lad, Charles O'Brien, auditioned and joined the group on lead guitar. By May, Richard Starkey, from the Dingle area, had been recruited to play drums, with another Old Swan lad and a friend of Charles, Walter Eymond, joining them on bass. Two quick name changes followed, with both Al Caldwell and his Raving Texans, and Al Storm and the Hurricanes being adopted. The band proved to be a very popular attraction with a good following, which led to plenty of bookings. The guys decided to purchase suits, and Johnny purchased his Antoria guitar before Walter acquired an electric bass guitar, making them the first Liverpool band to use such an instrument.

On their free holiday to Butlins, John was invited to sit in on guitar with Rory Blackwell and the Blackjacks for a couple of shows. They liked his style and offered him a place in the band, but John declined as he was going to be a star with his own band. Alan liked the name Rory and began to play around with it, before settling with Rory Storm. The band became Jett Storm and the Hurricanes, before deciding on Rory Storm and the Hurricanes.

Left: Johnny's Antoria guitar. (Courtesy of the John Byrne Collection)

Below: The insurance document for Johnny's Antoria guitar. (Courtesy of the John Byrne Collection)

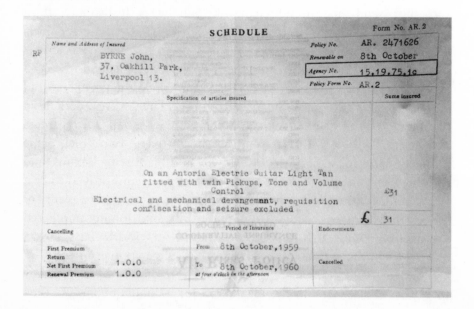

John chose the stage name 'Johnny Guitar' from the 1954 movie of the same title. The rest of the band adopted stage names too, with Charles O'Brien taking 'Ty Brien', Walter Eymond 'Lou Walters', and Richard Starkey 'Ringo Starr'.

A few days into the decade of the '60s, Johnny met a girl named Eileen Manson, who lived in the Formby area. They began to date and, although they were known to argue on a regular basis, they were soon going steady. A week after meeting Eileen, Johnny and the boys were kicked out of the Cavern Club for playing rock 'n' roll music.

The band was taking off and proving to be one of the most sought after local groups. They had a big following, and their popularity just kept on increasing. Butlins signed them for the summer season at the Pwllheli camp, and in October 1960 they opened at the Kaiserkeller club in Hamburg. A few days later the Beatles shared the stage with them, and the two bands became great friends. John returned from Hamburg with a leather jacket and crazy cowboy boots. He really was the rock star. John had very little luck with the first few cars that he bought; most had to be pushed down the hill of Broad Green Road to get them started. When he did manage to start the flash Jaguar, he crashed it into a petrol station hut when showing off to Eileen.

The band was playing all the major venues and the big events that Sam Leach was presenting. They had become very popular at the Iron Door Club and remained loyal to it until its closure. They returned to Butlins, Pwllheli, for the 1961 summer season and again proved a huge success. They continued to play the venues and big shows in Merseyside, along with a number of gigs further afield. In early 1963 they went out to France to play at the US bases, before returning for another summer at Butlins. This time they had been booked to appear in Skegness. Johnny's girlfriend Eileen had found herself a job at Butlins but was sacked when she was found staying in Johnny's chalet. The manager wanted to sack the Hurricanes as well but allowed them to continue when it was agreed that Johnny would live outside of the camp and only come in for performances. Eileen had to return to Liverpool or the deal was off. Johnny found a caravan and moved Eileen straight in. There are no rules for rock stars. Ringo also moved into the caravan, and it was here that two fellow musicians came looking for him. It was Johnny who answered the knock on the caravan door, and opened it to find John Lennon and Paul McCartney standing there. They wanted to speak with Ringo and, when he appeared, they offered him the job as the Beatles' drummer. He accepted straight away, and by the weekend he was gone.

Many accounts wrongly claim that the Hurricanes now fell apart. However, that was not the case, and they kept going just as strong as before. A succession of very good drummers joined them including Gibson Kemp, Trevor Morais, and Brian Johnson. They recorded 'Dr Feel Good', 'I Can Tell' and 'Talkin About You' on the stairway of the Rialto Ballroom on Upper Parliament Street for Oriole records. It was Keef who was with them when they returned to Hamburg to play at the Star-Club in 1963. In December 1963, Oriole released 'Dr Feelgood' as a single, with 'I Can Tell' as the B-side. Their fans bought the record, but it was never able to make a dent in the charts. By early 1964 Jimmy Tushingham had joined them; finally they had a long-term drummer who they could settle with. The band then went out to Barcelona, Majorca, and Ibiza on tour. They appeared on Spanish TV and radio while they were over there.

On their return, Rory saw Brian Epstein in the Blue Angel club. The conversation turned to why Brian had not helped the Hurricanes, and

Rory Storm and the Hurricans at Butlins, Skegness, 1962 (Courtsey of Margaret Byrne)

he agreed to take them to London and record a single. The song that Brian chose for them to record was 'America' and this left Johnny convinced that it had no chance of being a success. It was a party song that they had picked up in Spain. The song was recorded with 'Since You Broke My Heart' as the flip side. They did great versions of them, and 'America' has backing vocals and clapping from Brian Epstein, Ringo Starr, Iris Caldwell, and Shane Fenton (Alvin Stardust). However, Johnny was proved right and the single flopped. It was just not what the public was after.

During 1965 the guys performed in Germany, playing in Frankfurt, Dusseldorf, and Cologne. By the end of 1965, Johnny and Eileen had married, and in the summer of 1966 their daughter was born. The band had started to scale down the number of gigs that they took as they married and began to raise families. In February 1967, Ty collapsed on stage and died a few weeks later after complications with an appendicitis operation. It was all too much for the guys to carry on without their dear friend and the band split after a few more gigs.

Johnny had a family and took a job as a taxi driver to make ends meet. In 1970, a son was born to the couple. Johnny changed his job and became a milkman. He enjoyed this work and the customers liked him. When he later saw an advert for ambulance drivers, he applied and was taken on. From there, he went on to study and pass to become an emergency medical technician, or paramedic as they say today. He worked out of Crosby ambulance station and was very good at his job.

By the late 1970s, Johnny and Eileen had drifted apart and their marriage ended. Johnny moved into a flat in Green Park, Netherton. His job would see him call at houses only to find that the patient was a fellow musician from back in the day. On one occasion he took a call and arrived at the scene to find a hysterical lady crying about her son. On entering the house, he found it was one of his old friends from his music days who had sadly passed away. That experience really upset Johnny.

In the early 1980s, a call came over the radio of Johnny's ambulance and he answered that he would attend the address. When he got to the house he discovered an elderly lady who needed his assistance. He treated her, and afterwards, the lady's daughter asked him if he was Johnny Guitar from Rory Storm and the Hurricanes. He replied that he was, and the lady, Margaret, told him that she has watched the band at Butlins Pwllheli in the early 1960s. They met up again, began dating, and were married on 21 September 1984 at Waterloo registry office.

Rory and Johnny strolling along. (Courtesy of Margaret Byrne)

Johnny amassed a vast collection of Merseybeat memorabilia over the years: every poster, ticket, handbill, business card, and photograph – Johnny saved whatever he could. We have him and the rest of the Hurricanes to thank for saving those wonderful 1960 Kaiserkeller posters that Beatles fans love so much. He would show and sell many of his items various events, one being the Beatles convention at the Adelphi hotel. One year he was even invited to open the convention. Johnny's wife, Margaret, told of those times:

> Johnny loved talking to people and would spend time talking with anyone who approached him. I would help out on the stall, and there was always a queue of people wanting to have a small chat with him. At times, I would be hungry and wanting to go for dinner, but I would wait as Johnny would never just brush anyone off. Often, he would come to the conventions or other events, after a twelve-hour shift, yet you would never be able to tell. That is the kind of man that he was.

In 1987, the musical play *A Need for Heroes* ran at the Neptune theatre. Both Johnny and Walter Eymond came to see the performance. The interest that the play generated in the Hurricanes awakened something in Johnny, who decided to return to playing. He formed Johnny Guitar and the New Hurricanes and played at a number of charity events. The Merseycats charity was formed by a number of 1960s musicians in 1989. Johnny became a member and would perform at gigs for them. The new Hurricanes went down pretty well, with Johnny singing the songs that his old friend Rory had done in those early years.

In 1992, the play *The King of Liverpool* opened at the Playhouse theatre in the city. It was based on the life of Rory Storm, with Carl Wharton being chosen to take on the role of him. Johnny came to watch the play and was delighted with it, and his wife Margaret recalled that after the show Johnny went outside and did what he always did: take the poster from its holder as a keepsake. As he was doing this the former Coronation Street actor, theatre producer, and later Everton football club chairman, Bill Kenwright, shouted out: 'It's Johnny Guitar. I always wanted a pair of cowboy boots like the ones you wore'. Johnny later approached Carl Warton and asked him if he would consider performing as Rory Storm with the new Hurricanes at charity gigs. Carl agreed and came along to a few practice sessions before gigging with the band. He talked fondly about those days, playing alongside a legend such as Johnny, and of the fun that they would all have at Johnny's house.

During 1992, an American Beatles fan named Larry Wassgren made a visit to Liverpool. This was his second visit to the city, and, of course, he was coming for the Beatles. However, Larry had another wish. Being a guitar fanatic, he had come to admire Johnny Guitar and the Antoria that he had played. To meet Johnny was a dream of Larry's, but how could he find him? While in Mathew Street, Larry went into the Beatles shop and asked the guy behind the counter if he knew where he could find Johnny. He was told that he would be at the next day's Beatles auction and was advised to go along. Larry made his way there the following day. Johnny was there and was busy doing a lot of things. Larry decided to wait until everything was over before going over to say hello. He found Johnny very friendly and they talked for a while. Larry showed him a photograph in the book *Let's Go Down the Cavern* that showed Johnny playing his Antoria with John Lennon's Rickenbacker Kauffman Vibrola on it. Johnny was amazed and said, 'I had forgotten about that.'

Larry returned home and was kicking himself for not getting Johnny's number or address. However, his wife was able to locate it through international directories, and Larry gave Johnny a call. He was delighted to hear from him and the two chatted away about guitars and exchanged address details. In 1994, Larry returned to Liverpool and Johnny met up with him at the Adelphi hotel. Larry knew that Johnny was a big Elvis fan and had brought him a Presley's 78 disc, which Johnny was delighted with. They attended the Beatles auction, where Larry tried to bid on an original Gene Vincent Liverpool stadium handbill from the 1960 show, though the item sold for way more money than Larry was willing to pay. They went for lunch in the Cavern Walks, before Johnny invited him to his home. There, he showed Larry a suitcase that was full of posters and memorabilia from the Merseybeat days. Johnny then said, 'You really wanted that handbill didn't you?' Larry said he did, and Johnny produced one from his collection and told him: 'Here, this is for you.' Larry also got to play the Antoria guitar. Johnny plugged it into the vox amp that he had and handed it to Larry to play before going to get changed. When he returned to the room he said, 'Man! You Americans, you got that play Rock 'n' Roll in you'. Larry was delighted by this comment, even though he believed that Johnny was just being kind by saying it.

In 1992, Ringo Starr & His All-Starr Band had played at the Liverpool Empire. Ringo had said during the show that his old friend Johnny Guitar was in the audience. When Larry brought this up to Johnny he replied, 'I was not there, I would not pay any fucking money to watch Ritchie.' In fact, Johnny had remained friends with Ringo's stepfather, Harry Graves, and had driven him around to a number of places. Harry had told Johnny that he had tickets for Ringo's concert, though Johnny replied, 'If he wanted me there he would have invited me'. Johnny had popped into the Empire in the daytime when he was passing and came home laughing to Margaret, saying: '£5 for a programme the robbing git'. Despite this, Johnny was happy for Ringo and was touched when Ringo said that he was the first guitarist in Liverpool to have an attitude like Jimi Hendrix.

Larry and Johnny kept in touch by phone and letter. Johnny sent Larry photographs and even an original handwritten list of songs from a Hurricanes gig. Larry found a Reslo ribbon microphone, just like the ones that the bands used at places like the Cavern Club. He gave it to Johnny, who replied: 'Where the hell did you find that?' Johnny was delighted with it, and Larry found him two more.

On a trip to Liverpool, Johnny had set something up for Larry that he has never forgotten. He had arranged for Alan Stratton, who

Johnny still rocking with the Antoria in his home. (Courtesy of Larry Wassgren)

once played with the Kansas City Five, to take Larry to the former home of John Lennon – Mendips, in the Woolton area. When they arrived, Alan went and knocked on the door. It was opened by the owner, Ernie Burkey, who tended not to allow anyone into the house as the fans had become a nuisance over the years. However, he beckoned Larry in, and this star-struck fan spent two hours inside the house of his idol. As Larry says, 'That was Johnny, such a kind, and friendly guy.' He remains proud to have had Johnny as a friend.

Johnny continued to play at local charity events. He loved life, performing, and meeting people. He and Margaret had bought a caravan at Butlins in Pwllheli. They holidayed there for a number of years, where all the dreams had started for the Hurricanes in 1960. By then, of course, the site had mostly changed from those carefree days. Johnny became ill, and tests revealed that he had motor neurone disease. He carried on working for a short time and still played the

An original, handwritten Rory Storm and the Hurricanes set list. (Courtesy of Larry Wassgren)

gigs. As it took hold of him, he began to have trouble using his right arm. This meant that he could not strum his beloved guitar, and for Johnny, that was one of the most upsetting things.

In November of 1998, Johnny performed at his own retirement party. By now he could not use his right hand, so he shaped the chords of the songs as he sang. The following May, the 10th Merseycats anniversary show was held at the Bootle town hall. Johnny performed with his guitar virtually tied to him. He could not strum, but blew everyone away as he sang the classics from the Hurricanes days. This was probably Johnny's final appearance on a stage. Sadly, he passed away on 18 August 1999 at his home. Larry Wassgren had known that Johnny had become ill, though he never spoke to him about it. They talked about their families, guitars, the Hurricanes, and other Merseyside bands. It was Alan Stratton who rang Larry in America to inform him about Johnny's death. Over 300 mourners attended the funeral of this popular man, including his first wife Eileen. From a boy to a man he loved the guitar and rock 'n' roll – it never left him. And he will be remembered for being the kind, caring cool dude that he was.

Johnny Byrne and Cilla Black in the Cavern Club. (Courtesy of Margaret Byrne)

5

The African/Caribbean Influence

The Mersey sound, Merseybeat, or whatever you care to name it, was an incredible, unbelievable, and amazing period that I doubt can ever be repeated. Much is written and spoken of how skiffle, rock 'n' roll, and rhythm and blues were the templates that produced the sound that rocked Merseyside, Hamburg, Britain, and the world. However, there were many more types of music that influenced those musicians who blasted their way into the 1960s. Country, folk, and jazz music were very popular across Merseyside and were clearly adopted and used by many of the local beat artists, as were many other different forms of music. Liverpool has a vast cultural and musical history that was gained from its settlers, who came from every corner of the globe. Music has run rife through generations across both sides of the River Mersey. It is in the blood of the people and it was there a long time before the Beatles and the rest of the bands came along. It also continues to produce talent after talent from the area to this day. So, as you can see, Merseyside music was not created during the late 1950s or early '60s. It did explode then into something truly wonderful, but its roots began many years before.

Every area of Merseyside was producing talented bands and singers during these times. Nowhere else was like it; it was simply remarkable. However, one area, and in particular one set of performers, is oddly overlooked. Even though their influence upon the Merseybeat bands was of huge importance, very little is noted about it outside of their own community. The credit is simply never fully given, which is so wrong, as this is our history. Liverpool 8, Liverpool 1, Toxteth and Dingle is an area of diverse culture and home to some amazing musicians and singers. Billy Fury (Ronald William Wycherley) was from Toxteth, as was Gerry Marsden, Ringo Starr, and the Fourmost.

In fact, for most Beatles writers and fans, the only association with them to Toxteth is it being Ringo's birthplace. However, there is far more to it than that. The area had a lot of talent at that time that rarely receives a mention, and these people left a huge mark on the Beatles as well as other bands in their early days. I am, of course, referring to the black musicians and performers who could not only play the rock 'n' roll and rhythm and blues numbers, but who also brought ska, steel pan, and doo-wop, among other kinds of music. These three forms of music appealed to many of the Merseyside bands who took ideas from them. Steel pan and doo-wop were of huge interest to members of the Beatles, who watched, studied, and learned from the performers. Now, some people may agree with what I have written and angrily claim that the black performers have been given no credit. Others will nod their head and agree in a quiet manner, while some will probably deny that it happened. Then we have those who will be thinking: 'Doo-wop? Steel pan? Toxteth? Beatles? He is nuts.' All opinions are fair enough; each to their own. After speaking with many of the performers and researching all that I could find on them, it is my opinion – and mine alone – that someone, or something, was making it difficult for them to progress. However, this chapter is not here to talk about obstacles or attitudes. It is here to remember and celebrate a number of wonderfully talented people who entertained and influenced so many. But for now, let me just go off track a little.

If we are going to judge music by record sales then it is only correct that we go back to 14 March 1926, in the Toxteth area of Liverpool. On that day, at No. 13 Upper Pitt Street, Lillian Patricia Lita Roza entered the world. She was born to a Spanish father, Francis Vincent Roza, and a Liverpool mother, Elizabeth Anne Starkey. Lillian attended St Michael's School before moving on to the Granby Street council school, where one of her classmates was Jean Alexander, who most of us will remember as Hilda Ogden in the TV soap *Coronation Street*. Lillian was appearing in pantomimes by the age of twelve and toured the country, before returning to Liverpool to be with her family when the bombing raids became bad. In 1942, she took a job singing at the New Yorker in Southport, and it was here that she changed her name to Lita. Within a couple of months, she had saved enough money to take herself to London so that she could try and push her singing career. Lita was just sixteen at the time. That is pretty amazing for a period when women were not so respected for being independent. Within two weeks she had signed with the Harry Roy Orchestra. After marrying a year later and moving to Miami, Lita divorced and returned to the UK in 1950. She joined the Ted Heath Band and recorded with Decca. Her first single in 1951 was called 'High Noon, followed by 'Tears'.

In November 1952, the British singles charts had begun with Al Martino taking the first ever No. 1 position with 'Here In My Heart'. Record producers were all now eager to find success within the newly formed charts. Lita was asked by Decca to record the song '(How Much Is) That Doggie In The Window'. She refused, saying it was a load of rubbish, but the producer kept on trying to convince her that it would be a hit. In the end she agreed but said, 'I will sing it once, and once only'. She sang the song and it was recorded in one take. On 17 April 1953, the single reached the No. 1 spot in the British charts, thus making Lita the first British female singer and first Liverpool artist to reach the top of the hit parade. All this almost a decade before Merseybeat exploded. Not bad for a girl from Toxteth. However, Lita hated the song and, true to her word, she never sang it again. She did go on to make many more records and tour around the world in a wonderful career. Elton John would later comment about her: 'We just don't make singers like Lita Roza anymore.'

On her birthday in 2001, Lita unveiled the Wall of Fame in Mathew Street, which records all the No. 1 records recorded by Liverpool artists. On 28 November 2002, she was again in Liverpool, this time for a show at the Empire Theatre to remember the first broadcast of Radio Merseyside. Lita had now retired from singing for many years but she took to the stage and performed a number, thus ensuring that her final public performance was in her home city. Lita passed away on 14 August 2008 in London.

Of course, Lita was not a black person, but her musical culture was influenced by her Spanish father who played piano in a number of local pubs. It was this culture mix that spread its music across the city from north to south over many decades that gave the Merseyside area something different and special. So, who were the black performers who gave their ideas to the Mersey sound of the early 1960s? Probably one of the best known is Derry Wilkie, who fronted a number of bands and mixed with the Beatles. He was an incredible frontman who would put on a real, unrestrained show. Derry is covered in this book with his own chapter, so we shall move on to another man who had a huge impact on a couple of Beatles.

Odie Taylor, the brilliant jazz guitarist who people flocked to see play at the venues around south Liverpool including Dutch Eddies, the Nigerian Princess, Palm Cove, the Pink Parrot, Russells, Reeces, the Blue Angel, and the Bedford Social Club, just to name a few. Odie played with the Odie Taylor Combo and jammed with many a musician and bands; or, to be fair, most came hoping he would perform with them. Odie loved music and was a very unselfish man who would happily learn and encourage those who showed the desire. He also helped out many groups and singers by finding them work. Odie would do none of this for money as it was all for the love of music. He inspired so many people, not only those from within his own community but many from outside of it as well. They admired and respected him for his wonderful musical ability. They also provided him with the nickname of 'the Godfather'.

The Whitehouse pub on Duke Street was a venue Odie could regularly be found playing at. It was here that many a budding musician would come along to watch this talented man perform in the hope of picking up ideas that they could adapt into their own playing. Many of those who came to watch Odie at the Whitehouse pub would become Merseybeat stars, including John Lennon and Paul McCartney, who would both study his style. Musicians who played in the Odie Taylor Combo included Wayne Armstrong, Vinny Atherton, Tommy Brown, George Dixon, and Jimmy Hinds among others,.

Odie was born George Taylor, in Liverpool. So, where did the name 'Odie' come from? When he was a young boy he was given the part of one of the three wise men in his school nativity play. The line that he had to say was 'Oh lamb of God'. However, he said, 'oh the lamb of God', or, as it comes out in a Scouse accent, 'O dee lamma God'. Upon hearing it his teacher shouted 'ODEE?' and his classmates burst out laughing. From that day on 'Odie' stuck. He lived in Vine Street, off Myrtle Street. Later he moved to Pitville Avenue, off Rose Lane. It is claimed that he sometimes used the name 'Odie Lamb', which again goes back to the school nativity play. However, he did receive a number of letters addressed to 'Mr. Odie Lamb'. He is described as a lovely and very funny man who always made people laugh. He was a very good guitarist who could play jazz brilliantly, and also a great band leader with a very relaxed and fluent style. He later introduced soul numbers to the combo set and brought in Ronnie Joe Haynes as the singer.

By the 1980s, Odie had taken up driving a Hackney cab. One day he was parked second in line at the Liverpool airport rank. The airport was less busy back then so the drivers would hope for a good fare. A guy got into the first taxi and asked to be taken to Garston,

Odie Taylor. (Courtesy of George Dixon)

just a short distance away. The driver said he was not taking him there and told him to get the cab behind. Odie told the guy to get back in the first taxi as he had to take him by law. An argument then started and the taxi driver gave Odie a mouthful of racial abuse. Odie thumped him and knocked him to the floor, before saying 'Now you

Odie Taylor jamming away. (Courtesy of George Dixon)

will take him', and the driver did as he was told. In later life, he moved to Torquay to settle and enjoy his retirement.

In November 2000, Sugar Deen was given the Merit of Men award by Black History Month for his contribution to music in Liverpool 8. He was delighted with his award, of course, though he felt uneasy that Odie Taylor had not been recognised first and foremost. In fact, Sugar contacted the organisers of the awards and explained who Odie was and what he had achieved in his life. After a meeting, they decided to present Odie with a Men of Merit award at the prestigious Crown Plaza Hotel. Sugar phoned Odie to tell him the news and he was shocked, yet honoured. Odie and his wife came up to Liverpool to receive the award, even though he was very ill. Odie is still fondly spoken about in his old community, and is respected and admired by those who knew him.

Garry Christian, lead singer of the Liverpool band the Christians said:

My elder brother Roger was very good friends with Odie's son and that is how my family came to know Odie. Around 1972/73, before The Christians, Odie organised a soul competition and me and my brothers ended up singing in the final in London with him and his band. I have fond memories of Odie who was a lovely calm guy to be around.

Norman Frazer. (Courtesy of George Dixon)

Another influence to musicians were a band called the Casuals, consisting of Wally Quarless on lead guitar, George Dixon on bass, Norman Frazer on guitar, and Henry Deeson on drums. They were first-rate musicians, with all of the guys singing and harmonising together. When they first formed, Wally had suggested that they call the band the Tackaraddy All Stars, but George was having none of it and they finally settled on the Casuals. Their early gigs were around the Toxteth area, where they found regular work at the Bedford Social Club and the Masonic pub in Berry Street. The band's first ever gig is rumoured to have been at the Whitehouse pub on Duke Street. They became a regular feature at this pub and soon attracted a strong following. Like with Odie Taylor, up and coming musicians would come along to watch and learn from this talented band, Lennon and McCartney included, while George Harrison would also sometimes be present.

George Dixon had started singing with the big bands in the early 1950s. He became a regular singer at the Grafton Ballroom where he performed numbers such as 'That Old Black Magic' and 'Passing Strangers' with Mrs Wilf Hamer's Big Band. George spoke of those times saying,

> The guys playing the guitars around South Liverpool in the late 1940s included Odie Taylor, Eddie Jenkins, Robert Amoo, Wilf Johnson, Les Young, and the brothers Eddie, Johnny, and Powie Wenton. They would play songs such as 'Fly Me To The Moon', 'The Lady Is A Tramp', and 'The Girl From Ipanema'. You could not perform in pubs back then as they had to have a license to do so. The only two I knew of that had one were the 'Blue Ball' on Prescot Street, and the 'Cross Keys' in Earle Street. So, people would have a look-out watching as they played and sang. If the warning of 'Police Coming' was shouted, all the guitars would be hidden. If you wanted to be paid for singing then you had to play the big halls such as the 'Grafton' and the 'Wookey Hollow'.

George had served his national service before returning to Liverpool and teaming up with Wally Quarless. He noticed the skiffle sound that was taking hold and the bands that were springing up. Three guys with guitars were much cheaper than a big band, and George stated that it took little more than a year for those big bands to be almost wiped out within the city.

The Casuals had become one of the most popular acts at the Whitehouse pub, with many fans and musicians wanting to see them perform. The guys had noticed the musicians who kept returning to see them play and studying their chords. George recalled how Lennon and McCartney were often to be found at the pub watching the bands:

They were a skiffle band back then, and like other young musicians they
would come along and try to pick things up, chords, songs, style, etc.
So, when we heard that they had a gig in Tunnel Road, Wally Quarless
went along to see what they were like. He returned saying that they only
played three chords and did not know much.

Like a lot of young musicians, the Beatles were keen to learn and improve
their own playing. They were often seen watching the bands at venues
such as the Whitehouse, the Masonic, the Starline Club on Windsor
Street, and, of course, the Jacaranda in Slater Street. However, they were
not just coming into the area to pick up tips, for they were also forming
lasting friendships. They were regulars at the Unicorn café on Duke Street,
where musicians would hang out and chat about anything and everything.

By 1960 Norman Frazer had left the Casuals. Dave Stead became
the band's drummer, with Gerry Stewart coming in on saxophone,
thus allowing the group to play a wider range of music. They
remained regulars at the Whitehouse pub. George Dixon was able to
provide another Beatles-related story: 'In 1962, at the Whitehouse, we
were playing the song 'I Remember You' that Frank Ifield had a hit
with, and we could see John and Paul watching us closely. Not long

Norman Frazer and Wally Quarless setting up for a Casuals gig, with George Dixon
coming to join in. (Courtesy of George Dixon)

after we discovered that they were playing this song in their set. Well, they got that song from watching us'.

George also provided the story of a talent competition that almost led to him auditioning as a Beatle:

> I took part in a competition in the Lacarno Ballroom next to the Grafton. Cilla Black [Cilla White then] was in it as well, and I won. Afterwards, a blond guy approached me and told me how good my voice was. Later I realised that it was Bobby Willis, the future husband of Cilla. He told me that the Beatles had mentioned the possibility of adding a singer to their band and suggested that I go along and audition for them. I had no intention of doing that as they were still basically a Skiffle/Rock 'n' Roll band and I had no desire to play that type of music. A few months later I was out on the town with a friend when we decided to try and get into the Iron Door Club. Not the greatest idea for a black guy back then mind, I mean, even Derry Wilkie who performed at the club could come up against abuse and anger just for crossing over Victoria Street. We arrived at the club and knocked on that big door. A doorman answered, looked at us, and said, 'not today guys'. It was then that I blurting out that I had an audition with the Beatles. The doorman told me to come inside, so my plan was working and all I had to do now was slip off into the club. However, as soon as he had shut the door behind me he marched me off to the band room. Here he led me in and told the Beatles that I was looking for them. I stood there with John and George staring back at me. An awkward silence started to descend so I asked them if they were looking for a singer. John said to George 'are we looking for a singer?' and George replied that they were not. Then, John looked at me and said, 'You're the guy we used to watch in the Whitehouse pub?' I told him that I was and he responded with, 'You were good man'. I then thanked him and made my exit into the main part of the club.

By early 1964 the band had decided a name change was needed. When they were booked for a gig at the Cavern Club, Bob Wooler had asked them for the band's name. They told him they had not decided on one and he said, 'You can be called The Champions.' On 22 January 1964, the band, with a young Colin Areety joining them as a singer, appeared under that name of the Champions at the Cavern alongside Sonny Boy Williams, the Yardbirds, the Mastersounds, and the Pawns. During the evening, George sat watching a young lad playing guitar in one of the alcoves. He was brilliant, with his fingers running up and down the neck. George told him he was really impressed with his playing and the lad thanked him. That guitar player was Eric Clapton. After Sonny Boy Williams had performed, he was mobbed for autographs. He was wearing a bowler hat as he signed for the fans. George Dixon went over to him and asked him to sign a bit of paper. When he looked at it he saw the initials 'S. B. W.'; George asked Sonny why had he written that and he replied, 'My hand is fucking killing me from signing all the autographs'. The handbill from that evening's show is still available. Sadly, the ignorance of the times rears its ugly head on that handbill, where you can see written above the Champions' name 'The All-Coloured Combo'.

The Champions was never going to stick as a name and they had soon changed it to the In Crowd. The band remained very popular on the local scene up to 1965, when they split and Wally and George formed a new band under the same name with John Carney on drums and Tony Fayle coming in as lead singer. Carney left after a short period and was replaced by Tony Adams.

George Dixon recalled one of their touring moments:

We had bought an old 'Black Maria' van to get us around the country. It only had one seat in it and that was for the driver. The rest of the band had to find a space among the instruments and amps. Tony Fayle offered to drive everywhere so we let him. One day he was driving us when an awful noise exploded and the van stopped. The engine and blown and I asked Tony if he had changed the oil. He told me that he did and I asked him how often? 'Every year' was his reply. We almost hit him. We also found out that he had not passed his driving test, so that was the end of him running us around. Another time the van broke down just outside Swansea in South Wales. A friend came and towed us all the way to our next gig, in Edinburgh!

The band turned professional and toured around Europe. Steve Aldo replaced Tony Fayle on vocals and by 1968 the lineup consisted of Wally Quarless (lead guitar), Tony Lawrence (bass), Tony Adams (drums), and Steve Aldo (vocals). George Dixon had left to join the group Just Us, alongside Willie Wenton (Randy King) Ken Ross, Dave Stead and Eric Hanson. Wally Quarless and Steve Aldo would later join them. Just Us played cabaret clubs all over the country and went on tours of Germany and Greece. They also appeared on the TV talent show *Opportunity Knocks*, and on 6 April 2002 George Dixon appeared on *Stars in Their Eyes* performing as Ray Charles.

The In Crowd also later decided to try their luck on the TV show *Opportunity Knocks*, where they performed 'Blue Moon' and 'Walk Away Renee'. However, they finished second in their heat to a singing dog. They did end up with a recording contract when EMI signed them to their Deram label. They are believed to be the first all-black group to be signed by EMI. The band recorded a number of tracks, and in 1969 released the single 'Where in the World', with Tony Adams on lead vocals. The B-side was 'I Can Make Love To You', on which Steve Aldo took the vocal lead. The single never charted in the UK, but it should have done as it is a wonderful recording. It did, however, reach a high spot in the Netherlands.

The band carried on entertaining wherever they went. Members changed, and at one time the Beatles' former drummer Norman Chapman joined them. Colin Areety also played with them for a short time, while a lady named Rita Williams often joined the band for a few numbers, including the song 'It Takes Two'. Lynn Alli and Eric Hazz, among others, were also members of the band during its history. By the mid-1970s it was all over and the band split. Albie Donnelly and Dave Irving, who had played with the band in its last year or so, went on to form Supercharge. In December 1980, Wally Quarless sadly passed away – very close to the day that a guy who had eagerly watched and learned from him and other musicians in the Whitehouse pub was brutally murdered outside his home in New York, John Lennon. Wally has been described by those who knew him as a very funny guy with a matchless dry wit, a great guitar player – not just a strummer, but a musician – and whose Arabian oil prince imitation, played on shopkeepers, was nothing short of hilarious.

The Whitehouse pub is a restaurant today, and was once famous for having a Banksy rat painted on its exterior. It was once a major Liverpool music venue that attracted many famous people, yet little is mentioned about the pub and no tourists are directed to its importance. Not only was it a drawing point for the musicians who wanted to pick up tips and styles, but was also a showcase for many an aspiring singer. Doo-wop music was more popular to the young black lads of the Toxteth area than the skiffle that their white counterparts were producing. The Whitehouse pub, with its Sunday afternoon 'anyone can have a go' sessions, offered these young guys a place to practice and hone their skills. Basically, the pub was their training ground: somewhere they could perform to a live audience and feel the excitement of an appreciative crowd.

One of the youngsters who sang at the Whitehouse was Sugar Deen. He was born Rahman Abdul Deen on 30 September 1942 in Canning Street, Liverpool. His parents were Shitta Deen, born in Nigeria, and Janet Johnston, born in Scotland. His mother took the letter 'H' from his name and changed it to Ramon. His father took the family to live in Nigeria for a few years before bringing them back to Liverpool. On their arrival home, the council could only offer them a home in a tenement block off Scotland Road in the north end of the city – a predominantly white area. If you were black and went out of your community in the Toxteth area, you were likely to face racism. Parts of the Toxteth community have often been compared to the Harlem, where people lived separately to the rest of Liverpool in racial harmony. While living just off Scotland Road, some people subjected Sugar's family to racial abuse. In fact, his father took him to boxing lessons so that he could learn to defend himself. Sugar hated living in that area and was overjoyed when a home became available for them in the south end of the city and they returned to Toxteth.

The kids took his name 'Ramon' as 'Raymond', then they called him Ray. He attended St James School, where he joined the boxing team and became very good at the sport. The boxing gave him the nickname of 'Sugar Ray' and 'Sugar' has stuck with him ever since. His mother played the piano and she taught her children to sing and harmonise. Sugar put his first group – the Earls – together and they would practice at the Rialto Ballroom. They played one gig before Sugar decided it was not for him and joined a band named the Conquests. However, this was another short-term venture, and Sugar never gave up the search for the band that he wanted.

Sugar had a great voice and would practice singing doo-wop with his friends Lawrence Areety and Tony Fayal. They decided to form a group and call themselves the Shades, as they all went around wearing sunglasses. Being young lads, they would chalk their band name on any wall that they could.

One evening they were rehearsing inside the archway of Kent Gardens when Joey Ankrah came walking past and said, 'Man that sounds great, do you fancy forming a group?' Sugar replied with, 'We are already a group, we're called the Shades.' Joe told them that his house had a big basement where they could rehearse, so they opted to incorporate Joe and his brother Edmund into their band. After a few rehearsals, Tony decided that he was not happy with the arrangements

Slightly blurred, but another rarity. The Earls rehearsing on the stage of the Rialto Ballroom. Sugar Deen is centre of the group. (Courtesy of Ramon Sugar Deen)

and left. Tony was Sugar's friend, so he also chose to leave. Joe and Edmund Ankrah brought in Nat Smeda, Alan Harding, and Eddie Amoo, and kept the name of the Shades. Sugar, Lawrence and Tony teamed up with Eddie Williams to become the Valentinos.

Sugar recalled those early days in the Whitehouse pub:

Back then, the pubs would close at 3 pm. The pub had a lounge built on the side of it that is now gone. Every Sunday they would lock the doors at 3 pm so that people could enjoy a drink. Anyone could get up and sing or play with the band. We were all under pub age but we would go along and sing every week. It is where we learned our skills in front of an audience.

Sugar also remembered the many musicians who came from across the city to watch. In particular, two Beatles: 'The lounge had a small service hatch on one wall and this is where John and Paul first used to stand to watch the bands. I would see them and ask them to come in and Jam, but they always declined.' These young singers would also perform at the Masonic pub in Berry Street. This was the first pub to have a doorman; not because of trouble, but to keep the punters back when the pub was full.

The Valentinos proved to be a popular act on the local circuit and were soon being sought after by booking agents. This led to work around the country, including many working men's clubs where they sometimes faced abuse and had to share a bill with a racist comic. At some venues they would have to get the van driven to the club door before diving in and making a break for it. Every so often they had no option but to fight their way free from an angry mob. One vile compère disgustingly introduced them at one club as: 'Four of those black guys. You may like them but I don't.' Sugar Deen, however, assured the author of this book that the band enjoyed many good times while touring and that they outweighed the bad.

This was a very entertaining band with great voices and dance moves. They moved on to the big cabaret clubs where they would easily sell out gigs. Audiences loved them and talent spotters noticed them. This led to EMI signing them up to record a number of songs, though none of them were ever released. The guys soon realised that the record company had no real interest in them, and that left them to wonder why the offer had been made in the first place. On 23 January 1966, sixteen-year-old Stevie Wonder performed at the Cavern Club in Liverpool. In the audience were Sugar Deen and Colin Areety, who enjoyed the show so much that they jumped onto the stage and started backing the talented youngster halfway through one song. Someone shouted to them to get off the stage but Stevie said, 'No man, let them stay, that sounds good.'

The band was offered a tour of the US army bases in Germany. They accepted and received raving receptions from the troops whenever they performed. However, the guys had been stunned by the segregation rules that the military still had in place for their men. Even more shocking was the fact that they expected the Valentinos to abide by them. The tour proved a great success, though one evening brought Sugar Deen one of his most fearful moments ever.

The evening's performance was at the officers' club. On arrival at the club, they were told there had been a flood in the dressing room so they would have to use one of the offices instead to get changed for the evening's performance. While getting changed, Sugar heard a baby crying; the sound came from behind a screen in the office. When he looked behind the screen, there was a baby in a carrycot. He asked one

The Valentinos. (Courtesy of Irene Areety)

of the members of the group to go and get somebody and tried to cheer the baby up. A few moments later he heard a voice behind him say, 'Get your black arse away from that baby.' Looking up, he saw an officer brandishing what looked like a pearl-handled Magnum revolver. Sugar was marched outside, where the officer began to racially abuse him with every name that he could think of – all in full view of soldiers on the base. 'How dare you touch a white baby,' he roared, 'I ought to blow you away now and bury your body in the woods.' Sugar just stared at him in disgust while he was being abused, then flipped and screamed back 'You are a high ranking officer in the American army, I am a civilian, I'm not in your racist army. Black soldiers are constantly leaving for Vietnam and most are not coming back. They are giving their lives for your so called great USA. People like you are sick in the head, you racist b*stard. Unlike you, I don't see the colour of a man's skin I judge him by the content of his Character and personality, as was said by the late Dr. Martin Luther King Jr'. The officer replied, 'When on American territory, you'll do as I say boy.' Sugar just said 'f*ck you' and proceeded to walk back into the club, fearing the sound of gunfire as the gun was still pointed at him. 'This is not finished,' screamed the officer. Sugar just kept on walking.

During the evening's performance, that same officer sat in the front row and glared at Sugar throughout the show. Sugar could see his mind ticking over as he stroked his chin and glared. He was somewhat intimidated by his presence and wondered what the outcome would be. Speaking of this, Sugar said:

> After the performance me and the group were sitting at the so-called 'coloureds bar' having a drink when a voice shouted 'attention' as the same officer walked in and everybody in the place, black and white, stood to attention. The officer shouted 'at ease,' and everybody sat down again. He then approached me at the coloureds bar and glared at me for what felt like forever. Then, he called the barman over, who immediately jumped to attention, and said while pointing at me 'you feed this guy drinks' and on saying that he jammed a wad of dollars into a glass, and continued to say 'when that runs out you call me' and the barman said 'Sir yes Sir'. Another long glare towards me took place before he left the building … I can only assume that no one had spoken to him in that way before ever in his life, and would like to think that that racist episode gave him something to think about. I have to admit that I paid for one round of drinks then put the rest of the dollars in my pocket. I felt like he owed me something, but it bothered me throughout the night and it was as if I had received 30 pieces of silver. The next morning after breakfast I went looking for the officer to return his money but never found him anywhere on the base, and probably, that was the best outcome.

Author's note: Sugar Deen has kindly agreed to allow me to include the above story at my request. I believe that it is important for readers to understand what these guys, who just wanted to perform and do what they loved, had to face on a number of occasions. It also shows their own strength for having the ability to carry on in the face of such pressure.

The Valentinos returned to the UK and continued to tour. Eddie Williams had to leave for health reasons and was replaced by Vinnie Ismail, who had fronted the Liverpool band Vinnie and the Volcanoes. Vinnie was a brilliant guitarist who brought his talented playing and singing to the Valentinos. Vinnie is not a man that authors or historians should ever ignore. As you will see, he played his part in what was to come, though his credit and importance is far too often overlooked. He was born Vincent To on 9 July 1942 in Liverpool, later changing his name to Vincent Ismail. Vinnie grew up in the Toxteth area of Liverpool, where he took an interest in music. Once he picked up a guitar he was hooked, and soon became very accomplished on the instrument. By the start of the 1960s, Vinnie had formed his own group under the name of Vinnie and the Volcanoes. They consisted of Vinnie on rhythm guitar and vocals, Paul Pilnick on lead guitar, Robbie Eccles on bass, and Dave Preston on drums. They would practice at the Starlight club and Stanley House, where they could often be found rehearsing with the Chants.

The Volcanoes played the local circuit, where they got to know many of the other bands. John Lennon became a good friend of Vinnie and he could often be seen sitting with him asking Vinnie how to play a certain chord. Sometimes Paul McCartney would get involved, but it was mainly John who was fascinated by Vinnie's talent. In fact, it was Vinnie who showed Lennon and McCartney how to play the chords like Chuck Berry did. The Beatles were already playing Chuck's songs by this time but Vinnie showed them how to play the way Chuck did it, and Lennon was a willing student.

The band was managed by George Roberts and they found plenty of work before calling it a day in early 1963. Vinnie went solo, and there are many who believe that with the right person behind him he would have been a star. He also played with Liverpool band the Detours for a while. Think of the thousands of tourists who flock to Liverpool every year in search of the Beatles' history. Now ask yourself, how many of them would know the name of Vinnie Ismail? Or, for that matter, Odie Taylor, George Dixon or Walter Quarless among others. Yet these guys had a big influence on John, Paul, and George. It is rather sad to think that history is forgetting them.

With Vinnie in the lineup the Valentinos continued to tour, selling out the big cabaret clubs around the country. They even returned to Germany to play the US bases again. They decided to move to London to see if they could get noticed by the record producers. Denmark Street was the place to be and the band focused their attention on that area. Vinnie Ismail had played around this area with the Detours and the rest of the band were rather impressed that he appeared to know everyone around Denmark Street. One guy that he did know was the singer Gene Latter (born Arthur Ford in Cardiff). Gene arranged for the guys to come along to the EMI offices, where he introduced them to a number of producers. Sitting in an office, they were asked to sing a song. Vinnie ran outside to get his guitar from the car and they sang 'Do You Love Me'.

'Sounds great,' said a producer, and walked off. They sat in the office wondering what to do before being told that somebody would come for them soon. The lads had no idea what was going on and, after asking, were stunned to be informed that they were about to be signed up.

The band was given a date to record at Abbey Road studios. On their arrival they discovered that the Beatles were recording that same day, though they were told they were not allowed to go and see them. The guys were fuming at being banned from saying hello to their friends. The Beatles knew nothing about this, it was done by the studio staff. The recordings were done, though nothing was ever released, leaving the guys to believe that EMI had never really had an interest in them. By the 1970s, Tony Fayal had left to pursue a solo career. Barry Philbin joined the band, who had now changed their name to the Harlems.

They continued to tour and went out to perform at the American and British bases in Germany and Holland. Perhaps the scariest place they played was in Belfast. With Northern Ireland being classed as a war zone at that time, the band was paid extra money to perform there. The band had considered it a gamble going to play there, and it certainly was. They were booked to play at the Abercorn club and received a great reception there. One night as they left the club they were shot at by an unknown sniper. On another occasion, the guys were warned about going along to a party they had been invited to. They went anyway and while there a guy approached them and asked if they were staying at the Europa hotel. They told him that they were staying at a hotel opposite it as the Europa was too expensive for them, but they would use the Europa bar due to the 10.30 p.m. curfew being in place. The guy replied, 'Stay out of there on Saturday'. The lads from the band were unsure of what he was going on about: was he trying to scare or play a joke on them? They thought little more about it and returned to their hotel. On the following Saturday morning the guys were awoken by loud noises. Looking out of the window, they saw soldiers running up and down the street banging on doors and shouting at people to get out. The lads got dressed and left the hotel, even though the manager had told them that it was not safe to stay to do so. As they ventured outside they noticed a wagon parked across the road. Apparently, it had a bomb planted in it and soldiers were shouting to the guys to run as a machine slowly came past them. As they reached the end of the street, there was an almighty explosion that blew them off their feet. When they regained their senses they looked around and saw windows shattered and glass everywhere. The boys had a very lucky escape.

The Harlems. (Courtesy of Ramon Sugar Deen)

The Harlems brought in some great musicians to back them on stage, including Alan Sef, Keith Jones, Brian Nolan, and Mick Chong. They appeared on the TV show *Opportunity Knocks*, which led to Mickey Hayes becoming their manager and booking them some fantastic gigs. Mickey also managed to get them a contract with the DJM label. A date was given for a recording session in Oxford Street and the guys arrived full of excitement. While in the studio one day a

The Harlems. (Courtesy of Ramon Sugar Deen)

young lad came in to bring them refreshments, as he left the room a producer said, 'That guy writes some great songs. He'll be a star one day.' That guy serving them refreshments was Elton John.

A number of recordings were made and it was agreed that 'It Takes a Fool Like Me' would be released as a single, with 'There I Go' as the

The Undertakers.
(Courtesy of
Mave Atherton)

Undertakers Geoff
Nugent and Jackie
Lomax in Hamburg.
(Courtesy of
Mave Atherton)

The Undertakers.
(Courtesy of
Mave Atherton)

Geoff Nugent at the site
of the former Star-Club
in Hamburg. (Courtesy of
Mave Atherton)

Johnny Guitar's Antoria,
including a rare glimpse of
the back of the body.

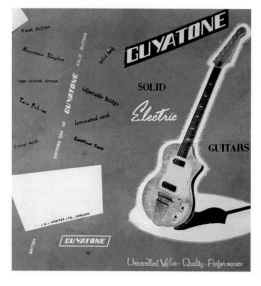

The Original leaflet that came with
Johnny Byrne's Antoria guitar.

Chuck Berry and Ted
Taylor. (Courtesy of Ted
'Kingsize' Taylor)

Jerry Lee Lewis and Ted
Taylor in the Star-Club
dressing room. (Courtesy of
Ted 'Kingsize' Taylor)

The Shakers in the Cavern
band room. (Courtesy of
Pat Trish Jones)

Phil Melia on stage at the Kaiserkeller in Hamburg. (Courtesy of Mave Atherton)

Billy Butler, Faron Ruffley and Geoff Nugent. (Courtesy of Mave Atherton)

Joey Ankrah, George Dixon and Sugar Deen.

Ivan Stax, Dennis
Fontenot and Paul
McCartney at LIPA.
(Courtesy of Ivan Stax)

Mark Singleton,
Ramon Sugar Deen,
Paul McCartney and
Joey Ankrah. (Courtesy
of Mark Singleton)

Johnny Guitair's original Hurricanes jacket,
still looking amazing.

Above left: Johnny Guitar's Kaiserkeller certificate signed by Bruno Koschmider.

Above right: Jackie Lomax at the Kaiserkeller, Hamburg. (Courtesy of Mave Atherton)

Johnny Guitar and his car. (Courtesy of Larry Wassgren)

Eddie Harrison from the Shakers.
(Courtesy of Pat Trish Jones)

Billy Kinsley and Victoria Jones at the
Lathom Club. (Courtesy of Paul Frost)

John Shell serving for the
USA Army at Fort Polk,
Louisiana. (Courtesy of the
Shell family collection)

Geoff Nugent doing what he loved. (Courtesy of Mave Atherton)

Taylor's Bar, Birkdale, Ted Taylor's former butcher shop. Ted Taylor, bar owner, John Frankland, Ant Hogan, Karl Terry and John Kennedy sitting.

Ted Taylor, Pam Birch, and Geoff Nugent in the Cavern Club. (Courtesy of Mave Atherton)

Above left: Johnny Guitair's 1960 Hurricane suit from Duncan the Tailor's in Liverpool. I was too scared to smooth it out for the photo in case it was damaged.

Above right: Johnny Guitar and Larry Wassgren. (Courtesy of Larry Wassgren)

Johnny Guitair's 1960 Cowboy boots that he bought in Hamburg.

The Hideaways performing at the Cavern Club, 2017.

Mojo Filter at the Cavern Club. (Courtesy of the Mojo Filter collection)

Val, Mary, and Sylvia of the Liverbirds in Gretal and Alfon's, Hamburg. (Courtesy of Mave Atherton)

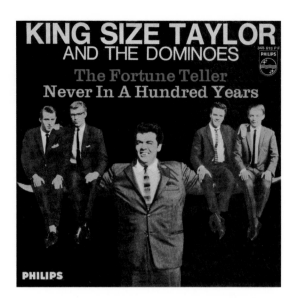

The Dominoes single 'The Fortune Teller'. (Courtesy of Ted 'Kingsize' Taylor)

The Harlems, for some reason listed as 'Harlem' on their single 'It Takes a Fool Like Me'. (Courtesy of Ramon Sugar Deen)

Mary Dolstal from the Liverbirds being interviewed at Fort Perch Rock. (Courtesy of Mave Atherton)

Geoff Nugent, Mary Dostal and Beryl Marsden at Fort Perch Rock. (Courtesy of Mave Atherton)

Johnny Guitar in his paramedic uniform with Larry Wassgren. (Courtesy of Larry Wassgren)

Deep in thought: Ivan Stax, Ramon Sugar Deen, Joey Ankrah and George Dixon surrounded by Joey's amazing artwork.

Above left: Martin Davies from the Shakers. (Courtesy of Pat Trish Jones)

Above right: Karl Terry. (Courtesy of Mave Atherton)

Frankie Connor at Fort Perch Rock, New Brighton. (Courtesy of Mave Atherton)

Kemp's Bar, Hamburg. Geoff Nugent, Brian Griffiths, Astrid Kerchherr, Bobby Thomson, Gibson Kemp, Veronica Thomson, Mave Atherton, and Nicky Crouch. (Courtesy of Mave Atherton)

Odie Taylor with Ramon Sugar Deen. (Courtesy of Ramon Sugar Deen)

Lou Walters (Walter Eymond) and Lee Curtis. (Courtesy of James O'Hanlon)

Victoria Jones. (Courtesy of James O'Hanlon)

Above: The author's adopted sisters: Mave Atherton and Iris Caldwell.

Right: Poster of the Valentinos. (Courtesy of Ramon Sugar Deen)

B-side. It was released on 18 February 1977, though their excitement was cut short by the lack of promotion for the single. Sugar Deen explained,

> We tried to buy copies of the single and nobody had it. John and Rita at the NEMS store in Liverpool ordered it for me and it finally arrived. I took it home but it would not play, it just jumped everywhere. NEMS ordered another copy and it was the same again. Then, people who knew us explained that their copies were jumping. The batch was faulty and very few of them ever played. If you have one that plays without jumping then you have a rare record on your hands.

The single had no chance of doing anything with all these problems, and the guys had to wonder if they were being messed around again. They did not record any more for DJM.

Tours continued, but in the end the guys split. It remains a shame that this talented band was not taken more seriously by the recording industry. Sugar went on to sing and tour Europe with the Les Humphries Singers in the early 1990s. He also recorded the album *Spirit of Freedom* with the band. Lesley Ankrah, the former wife of Joey Ankrah, also toured with the singers at the same time as Sugar. In the mid-1990s Sugar performed with a band called Good for the Soul alongside his daughters. They played at British army bases in Germany, entertaining the troops before they were sent out to Bosnia. His daughters Nicol, Natalie and Maxine, along with their cousin Shereen, played together as a vocal band named Onyx. Sugar's son, Ramon Judah, is a successful Reggae singer.

Ivan Stax had told Sugar about a music course that he was going to enrol in and Sugar decided to enrol himself. A year later, at the end of the course, they both received their diplomas. A company named Access to Music offered him a job as a music industry consultant. Mark Singleton, the guitarist from the band Afraid of Mice was also offered the post, with Ivan Stax Joining the firm around eighteen months later. The job consisted of a two-hour interview with young musicians and DJs in the job centre who had enrolled on a course called New Deal for Musicians. After accessing their standard, Sugar would then make the decision to which music course they would be best suited. If they were a DJ, he would place them on a DJ course in Benson Street Studios or on one off Bold Street run by Tony Bolland. If they sang or played an instrument, then he would send them to LIPA for a course run by Peter Hooton and a couple of guys from the

Ramon Sugar Deen performing in Liverpool. (Courtesy of Ramon Sugar Deen)

group the Farm. A lot of his time was spent at LIPA doing follow-up meetings with his musical clients. He would often meet up with his old friend Paul McCartney. Today, Sugar still sings and performs occasionally within the city. However, he says, 'I miss the guys every time that I gig. Somehow, it is just not the same. Bless them.'

Let us now return to the remaining members of the Shades, who Sugar and Tony had left to form the Valentinos. Joey and Edmund Ankrah had been raised by a father who was a church minister. He played the organ and encouraged his children to sing as well as taught them the art of harmonising. In March 1957, young Joey was working for a firm who made posters for the local theatres. His job was to deliver them. One day after making a delivery at the Empire theatre, he was making his way out of the building when he heard someone shout 'here he is'. Joey was then mobbed by a group of girls who had believed that he was Frankie Lymon. He found it rather amusing at the time and he did enjoy the music of Frankie Lymon and the Teenagers. He loved vocal songs and thought to himself, 'All I need is four other people and I could be in show business.' He never once doubted his ability to actually sing, and the boy was right. Along with his brother Edmund, Nat Smeda, Alan Harding, and Eddie Amoo, he produced something truly wonderful. These guys could really sing, often better than their American counterparts.

The guys continued to practice in the basement of the Ankrah family home and at Stanley House, the youth/social club on Upper Parliament Street. The club had four snooker tables and a football pitch in the rear yard. The young lads would play football with the older men and, in Sugar Deen's words, 'if you dirty tackled one of the older guys they would just smash you into a wall'. After the game people would go inside and listen to the band's practice. The Shades, or the Chants as they had become known, were drawing the attention of everybody at Stanley House with their brilliant doo-wop singing. The band sang acapella style and they were good – very good.

It is often claimed that the Beatles were the first band to back the Chants. However, Vince and the Volcanoes, who featured the brilliant rhythm guitarist Vinnie Ismail, were backing them almost a year before the Fab Four did. George Dixon from the In Crowd recalled the Chants:

We were playing regular at The Whitehouse pub and they would come in and ask us if we would back them at Stanley House. We had no interest and kept palming them off. However, they kept on asking so we decided to go along and do it. We set the gear up in Stanley House and the lads lined up together to play. We started playing the music and they began to sing. Well, we were blown away. Their harmonies were amazing, just perfect.

The Chants. (Courtesy of Joey Ankrah)

On 12 October 1962, Joey Ankrah made his way to the Tower Ballroom in New Brighton. As he walked towards the venue he bumped into Sugar Deen. Both guys were trying to get into the ballroom to watch Little Richard perform. They went to the stage door, knocked, and Brian Epstein opened it, then put his arm across the entrance before saying 'not tonight boys'. The guys protested, 'Come on Brian, let us in.' As they did, Ringo Starr came past and saw Joey and Sugar. He leant over Brian, grabbed hold of them and dragged them inside. They were in, and after watching the concert Joey got talking to Paul McCartney who asked him to bring the band along to the Cavern.

The following day, Joey Ankrah and Sugar Deen went along to the Adelphi hotel in Liverpool, where Little Richard was staying. Black people were still banned from staying at the hotel (unless they had a lot of money of course) so the sight of Joey and Sugar walking up to the reception must have worried the staff. They informed the receptionist that they were there for a meeting with Little Richard. Amazingly, it worked, and they were led upstairs to his room. Upon knocking, the door opened, and they could see Little Richard sitting in bed. He called to them 'come on in boys', and they entered. There sitting next to the bed were Lawrence Areety and Derry Wilkie, who had also managed to find a way in to meet their hero. As they all chatted, Little

Richard reached for a large book and opened it up. The middle had been cut out of it and was stuffed with pound notes. He said, 'I asked them for dollars and they gave me this shit.' The guys just looked on, stunned at the amount of money that was inside that book.

The Chants turned up at an afternoon Cavern session and the Beatles asked them to sing. They left the Beatles stunned with their version of 'A Thousand Stars' and were asked to perform that evening at the club. The Beatles informed Brian Epstein that evening that they would be backing the Chants. He was not happy and told them that he was refusing to allow them to do so. However, the band went against their manager and played the music for four songs that the Chants performed: 'A Thousand Stars', 'Sixteen Candles', 'Duke of Earl', and 'Come Go With Me' – the crowd went wild in appreciation for them.

The members of the Beatles convinced Brian to manage them, which he did, but under no contract. The Chants soon realised that his time was taken up with his other acts and so removed themselves from his management. They then signed a contract with Ted Ross, which led to a recording contract with Pye Records.

The band was going along well on the local circuit and were being backed by groups of the calibre of the Undertakers and the Big Three. Things began to move for them as they played around the country and went into the recording studio. They appeared on the TV show *Scene at 6.30* in August 1963, and just a month later their debut single 'I Don't Care' was released with 'Come Go With Me' as the B-side. This was followed at the end of the year with their second single 'I Could Write a Book', which used the flip side 'A Thousand Stars'. These were brilliant recordings, but neither single made it into the charts. The Beatles, when appearing on the TV show *Juke Box Jury*, had plugged their friends' second single, though the lack of exposure from the record company had left the band with a mountain to climb. However, back in Liverpool 8, the band was looked upon as heroes who had brought a lot of excitement, pride, and belief to their own community.

Two more singles followed in 1964: in May 'She's Mine' with 'Then I'll Be Home' on the reverse, and in September the wonderful version of 'Sweet Was The Wine' with 'One Star' as the B-side. Neither made the charts, but they were good enough. The lack of support from their label had once more hindered them. Pye Records had no idea what to do with the band, though a bit of effort promoting them would not have gone amiss. The song 'One Star' had been written by Eddie Amoo as a tribute to Stanley House on Upper Parliament Street.

The Chants at the Cavern, with Cilla Black watching from side of stage. (Courtesy of Joey Ankrah)

The Chants broke themselves free from Pye and went on to record a number of singles with different labels, including 'Come Back and Get This Loving Baby'/'Love Light' on Fontana in 1966, 'Ain't Nobody Home'/'For You' on Page One in 1967, 'A Lover's Story'/'Wearing a Smile' on Decca in 1967, 'A Man Without a Face'/'Baby I Don't Need Your Love' on RCS Victor in 1968, 'I Get The Sweetest Feeling'/'Candy' on RCA Victor in 1969, 'Love Is a Playground'/'Sophisticated Junkyard' on Fresh Air in 1974, and finally, 'I've Been Trying'/'Lucky Old Me' on Chipping Norton in 1976. By the time that the last single had been released, the Chants had come to an end. It remains a crying shame that these boys did not hit the big time. They recorded enough tracks to cover an album. It would be nice to see someone put one together one day so that many others can enjoy their talent.

Joey and Edmund Ankrah along with Joey's then wife, Lesley, went on to form the group Ofanchi, who appeared on the TV show *New Faces* before signing to Pye Records, with whom they recorded two singles: 'Sweet Surrender'/'Shall I Wait For You', and 'Don't Pity Me'/'Come On Back'. They were later signed to RCA and released three more singles: 'That's the Way (How Love Grows)'/'One More Minute', 'Making The Best Of a Bad Situation'/'Gonna Do My Best To Love You', and 'Let's Make Love'/'Yesterday's Affair'.

In 1970 Eddie Amoo's younger brother Chris formed a band with his friends Dave Smith, Kenny Davis, Ray Lake, and Eddie Ankrah. They had gone through a number of various names, including South Corner Triad, Sophisticated Soul Brothers and Vocal Perfection. Eddie Amoo would help out his brother's band with their development and began

Ofanchi. (Courtesy of Joey Ankrah)

to compose songs with his brother for them to use. They were a very popular band on the circuit, though Eddie Ankrah and Kenny Davis left the group, who then became a trio. The band signed with Tony Hall Enterprises and it was Tony himself that came up with the name the Real Thing after seeing it on a Coca-Cola advert. The band released their debut single 'Vicious Circle' in April 1972 under the Bell label. It never charted but, after a successful appearance on the TV show *Opportunity Knocks*, they were signed to EMI and toured as backing singers for David Essex and sang backing vocals on a number of his records.

Five singles followed over the next two years but, again, none of them charted, though they did appear on *Top of the Pops*. Eddie Amoo left the Chants to join the Real Thing after they left EMI. The band signed with Pye Records, the company that had signed the Chants. Two singles followed during 1975, though neither found that elusive breakthrough. Tony Hall then hooked up with Ken Gold and Micky Denne, who suggested two songs that they had written may be suitable for the Real Thing. The band agreed to record them and on 26 June 1976 their version of 'You To Me Are Everything' went to No. 1 in the UK charts, where it stayed for the next three weeks. It was a fantastic recording by the guys and it shot them to fame worldwide. This was followed up by the second Gold/Denne song 'Can't Get By Without You', which reached No. 2 in the charts and firmly established the band. Singles, albums, tours, and TV work all followed. They became a very popular and much sought after band. Finally, an all-black British band had smashed down the wall and broken through in the UK music industry. These wonderful, talented singers deserved all the success that came their way.

As with other bands, the Real Thing never lost their roots or love of their city. They remained based here and bought houses in the area. A number of singles and albums followed over the years, but it is their 1977 album *Four From Eight* that really showed their serious musical side and produced a number of songs based on their experiences of living in the Toxteth area, a place they are all very proud of. The songs 'Liverpool 8', 'Children Of The Ghetto', and 'Stanhope Street' are superb recordings that highlight the trying times and show the bands pride for the area. However, Pye Records refused to allow them to name the album 'Liverpool 8', so it was called *Four From Eight* (four lads from Liverpool 8). In 2008, Ringo Starr had no such problem when he released his album, and a song, that were both titled 'Liverpool 8'.

The Real Thing are still performing today, entertaining and thrilling the audiences who still flock to see them. They were the band that broke the mould and paved the way for other black British artists. They have inspired many people and have stayed loyal to the city that they love. They helped to put Liverpool music back on the map after those exciting days of the 1960s had faded. They deserve a lot of credit for what they have achieved.

Harold Adolphus Philips was born 15 January 1929, in Laventille, Trinidad. His father, James, was from Venezuela and worked as a butcher, while his mother Edna had been born in Grenada. He loved music and took up the guitar at an early age. In 1943, at the age of just fourteen, Harold decided that he was going to fight in the war that was raging across Europe. He took the passport of his brother Thomas and managed to enlist himself in the RAF. He came to England where he was first stationed in barracks in Westminster before being sent for training at Filey in north Yorkshire. He was then stationed in Burtonwood near Warrington, where he spent the remainder of the war. He worked as part of the aircrew as a flight engineer. It is amazing that his age was never spotted, especially when you consider that most of the men he worked alongside were much older than him. Did the RAF turn a blind eye? Who knows. The airmen would travel into Liverpool for nights out when on leave. Harold liked to attend the Jokers Club on Edge Lane as they ran talent competitions that he would enter. It was here that he noticed a young lady named Helen Agoro, who also sang in the competitions. They became friendly and began dating. In 1947, when Harold was demobbed and returned to Trinidad, he and Helen kept in touch by letter.

In Trinidad he again took up his love of music, and started singing calypso on the street corners. He would sing songs about the latest news as many people could not afford newspapers. He would also sing them the latest gossip from the area. He teamed up with Aldwyn Roberts (Lord Kitchener) and Egbert Moore (Lord Beginner) to play calypso music. Harold had written a song in which everyone was a cigarette character, one of which was called Woodbine. People would shout out to him 'Woodbine' or 'Lord Woodbine' and the name stuck. The names were all a skit on the aristocracy. They were becoming titled lords through their skill of calypso music. This is where Harold got the name 'Woodbine', and not, as is claimed, because he smoked woodbine cigarettes. In fact, he never smoked woodbines at all.

He had a fondness for the American cigarettes that he had discovered at the Burtonwood base and enjoyed the occasional cigar.

The three musicians toured through Jamaica with a band called the Young Brigade, before hearing of a ship that was taking people to England. They decided this was their chance of a new life and raised the money for the passage. Also on the ship, and in the company of the three men, was Wayne Armstrong, who later went on to play the double bass with the Stevens Band and with the Odie Taylor Combo in Liverpool. On 22 June 1948, the SS *Empire Windrush* landed at Tilbury Dock in London. The guys were part of the first wave of Caribbean immigrants to arrive in the UK and were making history. Harold stayed in a shelter at first in Clapham, before moving on to Shropshire to take up an offer of work as a machinist. Kitchener and Beginner stayed in London and became well known for their music.

Harold soon tired of the nitty-gritty life of factory work. He formed a new band that went by the name of Lord Woodbine and his Trinidadians, who became one of the very first calypso bands to tour around the country. When the band came to Liverpool he sought out Helen Agoro. They began to date again, fell in love, and married at St Michael's in the city church on 19 November 1949. Liverpool became Harold's home, and the place he and Helen raised their eight children. Helen was a great singer and she performed with Harold's first Liverpool band the Cream of Trinidad.

With a family now to feed, Harold took a number of jobs. However, that musical excitement remained within him and he came up with an idea to make it pay. He took over a shop in Smithdown Lane and moved his family into the rooms above it. The shop had two large windows either side of the door. Helen suggested that she could use one side of the shop to sew and sell things as she was an experienced milliner. Harold decided that the premises would be better suited being turned into a club. This is what happened, and his own band played here. In 1955, he sold the club to another businessman, which leads to the speculation that the club Harold started became the Palm Cove Club, though this remains uncertain. By the end of the decade he had opened another club at No. 80 Berkley Street under the name of the Colony Club. Harold also put the skills that he had learned with the RAF to good us, by taking a civilian job at the US Airforce base at Burtonwood, near Warrington.

When Lord Kitchener opened a club in Manchester in the mid-1950s, Harold would often go along and play with the band there. The brilliant Winston Spree Simon also played at the club for a while and Harold played alongside him a number of times. He was also happy to learn from Spree, who showed him some valuable skills to enhance his own steel-drum playing. Harold is also known to have played in a band for a short period with Spree, an African drummer named Bongo, and guy called Victor. They played around the UK and Ireland. The late 1950s had also seen the formation the All Caribbean Steel Band, of which Harold was a member playing the tenor drum. Other members included Gerry Gobin, Otto, Everett, Bones, and Slim. Harold played at the ceremony for the 1958 British Empire and Commonwealth games. It is probable that it was the All Caribbean Steel Band that played alongside him.

This was a very popular band with a great following. They played a number of venues on a regular basis, and it was at one of them that they first began to notice two white musicians who would watch them intensely. It was not at the Jacaranda that they first became aware of them, as is claimed so often, but at the Joker's Club on Edge Lane. Of course, many of the young musicians would come to watch them but these two stuck out as they watched everything that the band did. When Harold had bought the New Colony Club, he left the Steel Band to give himself the time to run it. He sat in with them a number of times and gave them a few gigs at his club. One venue that they appeared at regular was a Greek club on Princess Road. It was here that Allan Williams noticed them playing and offered them more money than Harold was paying to play at the Jacaranda. Basically, he poached them, and Harold, still being the bandleader, went along to Williams' club to find out what was going on. Fortunately, the two men struck up a good friendship that led to a business partnership.

When the band took up residence at the Jacaranda club, the two white muso boys stuck out once more. The two guys in question were John Lennon and Paul McCartney, who would ask to have a go on the steel drums and try to join in with the band on guitars. The band members began to suspect that these two were trying to learn their black sound and became annoyed with them following them around and trying to play their instruments. However, as time passed they got to know them and they all became friends. The guitarist Zancs Logie would sometimes get up and play with the band. He is another person who John Lennon asked to show him the chords that he played. Zancs was happy to oblige and John was a willing pupil. Once he had mastered a number of the chords, Lennon was eager to jam with the band whenever the opportunity arose. Paul McCartney's main interest lay in the steel drums, and, just like John, he was a willing pupil.

By early 1960, 'Woody' – as Harold was known by everyone – was no longer joining in with the band due to business commitments. They now changed their name to the Royal Caribbean Steel Band and within months had taken up an offer to go and play in Hamburg, Germany. They were a Liverpool-based band and that makes them the first Liverpool band to go out to Hamburg. The importance of how calypso music and the steel drum influenced Lennon and McCartney is overlooked far too often; they clearly loved the music and learnt from it. That is to their credit, and that was their talent: learn and adapt. They were not born songwriters, they studied and put the effort in. Their willingness is admirable. Of course, calypso cannot take the full credit for what was to come, though it played its own part in something that became truly wonderful.

Allan Williams and Woody decided to open a club together: the New Cabaret Artists' Club in Upper Parliament Street – such a grand name for a strip joint. Woody became the manager of the Jacaranda when they became business partners. They both helped out the Beatles – who consisted at the time of John, Paul, George and Stuart Sutcliffe – whenever they could, giving them a few gigs at the Jacaranda and the New Colony Club. The Beatles were also allowed the glamorous gig of backing 'Janice the stripper' as she removed her clothes at the New Cabaret Artists' Club. They spent so much time with Lord Woodbine that people began to call them 'Woody's Boys'. Gerry Gobin was contacting Woody from Germany and telling him to get over there as he would love it. He also suggested that the Beatles could benefit from playing there. Do you read about Gerry Gobin in the Beatles books?

Woody and Williams both took the trip to Hamburg and were amazed by the scene there. Their meetings with local club owners led to Williams becoming an agent for Bruno Koschmider, where he would send out local bands to play in his local clubs. This, of course, resulted in the Beatles – now with Pete Best on drums – going over to play at the Indra and Kaiserkeller clubs. It was Woody who bought the Volkswagen van that he and Williams drove the Beatles to Hamburg in. Woody had performed in Hamburg during his trips there. However, he often liked to push barriers with the words in his songs and this sometimes got him into trouble.

In 1961, Woody took over the management of Williams' Blue Angel club. From time to time he also played with a band named the Rhythm Calypso Boys. He was great friends with the sculptor Arthur Dooley, who was just two days younger than him. In the late 1960s, Arthur asked Harold if he would pose for a sculpture that he wanted to produce, titled 'The Black Christ'. Arthur had wanted to use his friend as the model due to him having an ethnic background that covered four continents. He told Harold that his face would represent the world. Harold agreed to be the model and Arthur took a mould of his face. In 1969, the statue was unveiled upon the outside of the Methodist church on Princess Road. The correct name for the statue is *The Resurrection*, though people call it 'The Black Christ'.

In 1975, Allan Williams released the book *The Man Who Gave the Beatles Away*. Harold did not like how he had been portrayed within the book, which led to some anger between the two men. Woodbine was not just a friend of the Beatles. He had taken them under his wing when they were looking to progress and helped them in every way that he could. They looked up to Woody and wanted to be around him. Williams would later give Harold the credit he deserved by saying that, without Woodbine, the Beatles would not have made it. What Williams said is a tad over the top, but it does reflect the influence that Harold had on the young Beatles in those early days. This brings us back to the compilers of Beatles history who tend to underplay the role of Lord Woodbine. It is very simple, both Williams and Woodbine played their part in Beatles history. However, many writers have chosen to push Williams to the front of the story while relegating Woodbine to a bit part. Both men were partners. If Williams was the Beatles' manager, then so was Woodbine, and that is how he saw himself. Remember, the guys knew Woody before they knew Williams. They had followed him and the Steel Band to the Jacaranda club where they had met Allan. A business partnership was good for both men; they needed each other and both contributed. Woodbine brought his knowledge and contacts of clubland and music, and this was no doubt a benefit to both Williams and the Beatles. To be fair, Harold had never been bitter about his association with the Beatles being neglected. He was proud of them and, unlike some, did not try to cash in on his former friends.

Harold ran a number of shops over the years and was regularly seen at local auctions where he would buy items to sell on. He really was a man of initiative. He was a painter and decorator who was employed to give a lot of the local clubs a makeover, such as Dutch Eddies and the Gladray. He made cocktail bars for the clubs, fixed cars, TVs and most things that were broken. He worked as a barber, taught painting, and made a hot pepper sauce that he sold and gave away to people. In the 1970s, he taught painting and decorating to youths. He was also a very skilled carpenter. He would lend a hand to many people – very often free of charge. He was very active as a socialist and became a bit of a philosopher. He could turn his hand to anything and was very much a part of the culture of Liverpool 8.

In 1992, Harold was invited along to the Liverpool Playhouse for the opening night of the play *Imagine*. No mention of him was made during the play, yet Harold would never worry about not being recalled in Beatles history. After all, he was used to it, and it was writers and not the Beatles themselves who had opted to ignore or underplay his role in books, articles, and documentaries. What did hurt him at that play was the photograph that was used as a backdrop. It was the famous Arnhem Oosterbeek War Cemetery photo that was taken of Woody, Williams, and the Beatles as they travelled through Holland towards Germany during that 1960 trip. To his dismay, as Harold stared at the image, he saw that he had been airbrushed out of it. We can only imagine the slap of insult that he must have felt as he sat in the theatre. When asked about it, he did later mention that maybe the Beatles' publicity people did not want a black man associated with their history. He was, however, very moved when Paul McCartney mentioned him during the anthology mini-series in 1995.

In 1998, the Windrush Foundation and BBC Radio Merseyside paid for Harold to return to Trinidad with the journalist Tony Henry as part of the 50th anniversary of the SS *Empire Windrush* first sailing. Harold had lost touch with a lot of relatives in the previous few years and was terrified of what he may find. He sadly discovered that his brother, Thomas, had died a few years earlier. Nobody had informed him of his death, and Harold was so distraught that the interviews with him were cancelled. The BBC4 radio programme *A Long Way From Home* was the result of his trip to Trinidad. He also met with Prince Charles during the Windrush 50th anniversary. Tragically, on 5 July 2000, Harold and Helen both died during a fire at their home in Liverpool.

In 2008, Paul McCartney mentioned in an interview with *MOJO* magazine that the Beatles were friends with a lot of black people from Liverpool, and that Derry Wilkie and Lord Woodbine were mates that they hung around with. Woody would have been proud to have read that. In 2014/15, the 'black Christ' statue on Princess Road Methodist Church underwent a renovation that would preserve it for many years to come. A strange thing is that the plaque that was put up at the same time to remember Arthur Dooley is dated 5 July 2015. That is fifteen years to the day that his friend, and model for the statue above the plaque, passed away with his wife.

Colin Areety played with a number of the local bands, including the In Crowd, the Contrasts, the Dennisons, the Almost Blues, and the Micheal Henry Group. He also had a successful solo career and proved popular on the cabaret circuits. Colin went on to perform at Caesar's Palace in Las Vegas and toured with the Supremes. He recorded a number of singles during the 1970s, which included 'Dancing Child'/'All For You', 'Poco Joe'/'To Give All Your Love Away', 'Holy Cow'/'I Can't Do It For You', 'Power To All Our Friends'/'That's What You Mean To Me', 'If Loving You Is Wrong I Don't Want To Be Right'/'One Night Affair', and 'Baby You Don't Know How Good You Are'/'Freedom Fighter'. In 1982 he released his final single 'Love and Pain'/'Midnight Disco Train'. Colin had attended St Vincent's School with Tony Crane, who went on to play with the Merseybeats.

One band that started around 1965, and provided a rather sweet story, were called the Essence. They consisted of Jeanne Renner,

Colin Areety and Albie Donnelly. (Courtesy of Albie Donnelly)

George Quarless, Roy Jenkins, Eddie Ankrah, and Eric Scott. The band performed a few gigs and rehearsed in the Ankrah's basement on Parliament Street around the same time that the Chants, and the In Crowd, along with numerous others who were leaving their musical marks. Tony Fayal and Walter Quarless would coach them at times. When the band members Jeanne and George fell in love and decided to get married, that was the end for the group. For a time they had lived the dream that had been inspired by the doo-wop entertaining of the local lads, along with the American music that was quickly becoming available to them through NEMS, and the GI's who brought the music with them from air and army bases around the country.

Edward Bedford (Edward Alban Jean-Pierre Bedford) performed under the name of Steve Aldo. At the age of thirteen, during a family holiday in the Isle of Mann, he sang with the Ivy Benson Band. Within a year, Steve was getting up to perform a number or two with some of the local bands at their gigs. He also sang with Howie Casey and the Seniors on many occasions. Steve became the frontman with the Challengers, before singing with Kingsize Taylor and the Dominoes for a few months in Hamburg during 1963. He performed with the Griff Parry Five, the Nocturnes, the Fix, and the Krew, before turning his attention to a solo career. He was signed by Decca and in December 1964 he released his brilliant version of 'Can I Get a Witness', B-sided by 'Baby What Do You Want Me To Do'. Steve toured with the Beatles on their final UK tour in December 1965. In April 1966, he released 'Everybody Has To Cry'/'You're Absolutely Right' on the Parlophone label. Neither single charted, though they remain fantastic recordings. He also sang with the Liverpool bands the In Crowd and Just Us, among others.

Tony Fayal was another talented singer who had started out by performing with the Odie Taylor combo. He was a forming member the Valentinos and later sang with the In Crowd. Tony toured around the country performing on the big cabaret shows and spent time comparing alongside Marti Caine. He was also a regular singer at the Wooky Hollow club in Liverpool, where he was also asked to compère shows on many occasions. Tony later performed regular gigs at the Labour club in Stockbridge village.

The Wenton brothers – Bernie, Willie and Bobby – are already mentioned within this chapter as members of various bands. They hailed from a musical background as their father Powie was himself a performer. Powie was a talented guitarist and singer and his children were highly influenced by him. These boys had a talent in their own right that can clearly be seen by the lists of bands and performers that they played alongside. What was also very evident was how close they were to one another and the pride that they had whenever they would perform together.

Bernie was a member of the band the Pride and Joy, who's name changed to the Pride and Joy Buzz Band, before becoming Bernie and the Buzz Band. They were a storming soul band who released the brilliant 'Don't Knock It'/'When Something Is Wrong With My Baby' in March 1968 on the Deram label. This was followed in September of the same year with the single 'The House That Jack Built', which was brought out by Decca.

Willy had played with the group Shuffler Sound and Bobby and Bernie would later join the band. Willy also sang with Stateside Review and toured the UK, Germany, and Greece with the band Just Us. They also appeared on the TV talent show *Opportunity Knocks*. When the three guys performed together as the Buzz Brothers, people would literally queue around the block whenever they were on. Their singing and dance routines were nothing short of brilliant. However, fame had passed them by and they took day jobs as they started their own families. They still performed and toured at times, after all, you cannot keep talent down. During the late 1970s, Bernie and Willy toured with Chris Rea as his backing vocalists. They also appeared

Bernie Wenton, Ivan Stax, and Willy Wenton at the Philharmonic pub, Liverpool. (Courtesy of Ivan Stax)

with Bobby in the Channel 4 TV documentary *A Place in the Sun* and Bernie sang on one of the *Class Of '64* albums.

Bernie had tried many times without any success to get himself onto *Opportunity Knocks* to gain exposure. When the chance arose, he applied for, and was accepted onto, a relatively new talent show called *Stars In Their Eyes* – a talent contest in which contestants impersonate stars through singing. Bernie entered as Nat King Cole and sang the song 'When I Fall In Love'. He made it to the final, where his incredible performance saw him crowned the winner of the show. An emotional and slightly stunned Bernie told the delighted presenter Leslie Crowther that 'fairytales really do come true'. His victory shot him to fame and the offers came flooding in. He toured the UK and Europe and realised an ambition of his when he sang with a big band orchestra. As an added bonus the orchestra was full of musicians who had actually worked with Nat King Cole. He was also delighted when he met Freddie Cole, the brother of Nat.

However, no matter how much limelight he was thrown into he still remained the same down-to-earth guy that he always had been. He turned down gigs that would have taken him around the world and offers from cruise companies as he did not want to spend so much time away from the family that he loved. One day when he walked into the Royal Liverpool Hospital he was approached by a surgeon who appeared to be fully dressed for the theatre. He said to Bernie, 'You're Nat King King from *Stars in Their Eyes*,' before shaking his hand. That really touched him.

Bernie always believed that the Liverpool 8 scene was just about to explode when the Beatles broke. He thought they were great but always considered their phenomenon at that time to be a massive shame for the L8 music, which was from then on more or less almost totally abandoned by the producers.

Sadly, Bernie was diagnosed with terminal cancer. On 20 April 2006, Chris Rea played a gig at the Philharmonic hall in Liverpool. A note was left there for him informing him of Bernie's illness in the hope that he may respond and give Bernie a boost. Chris performed his show before making his was to Bernie's house in the Toxteth area. Bernie was delighted, and the two guys sat chatting about the old days when they had toured together. Just three days later, Bernie lost his fight. Sadly, Bobby passed away in 2016.

Bernie's son, Bernie Jr, was a talented singer and guitarist who performed with his sister Melissa. Sugar Deen spoke about young Bernie who, in 2016, sadly passed away far too young. 'Young Bernie,

Bernie Wenton. (Courtesy of Melissa Wenton)

known as Buzz, used to attend the Charles Wootton Music Workshop and obviously received extra tuition from his father Bernie Snr, He gigged as a duo with his sister Melissa. He had a great voice and you couldn't meet a nicer guy.'

I have yet to find a bad word said or written about the Wentons, which speaks volumes about them. They just loved to do what they did best: perform and entertain – and they most certainly did that.

George Roberts, was the manager of Vinnie and the Volcanoes between 1960 and 1962, before taking over the Clayton Squares. He was one of the first people who was able to book gigs for black musicians outside the L1 and L8 areas of Liverpool. He also witnessed, first hand, Vinnie Ismail showing Lennon and McCartney how to play the Chuck Berry chords. George went on to say:

> The influence of the Liverpool 8 area on musical development spread beyond its tightly controlled 1950s borders to reach and inspire a great number. It was not just the Beatles in their embryonic form, but many of Mersey Beats white musicians, a number who went on to find fame, who came to sample the exotic nature of our particular cultures. It is my belief that the culture of Liverpool 8 formed the basis and backbone of Mersey Beat. McCartney was hanging out in Liverpool 8 from when he turned up at the Liverpool institute school at the age of eleven. Lennon was around the area from the age of seventeen when he pitched up at the college of art. Once they had left their homes in the sticks, Liverpool 8 became their new home. All its clubs, people, and atmosphere seeped into their bones long before they became famous. One could easily argue that Liverpool 8 had a profound influence on them both from a very early age. I lived at 54 Huskisson Street, and Alan Williams lived at number 58. That is where they all left for Hamburg from, driven by Lord Woodbine [aka Harold Phillips] in their beat up old van. They may never have found the sound that they developed had they not spent a lot of time in Liverpool 8 as well as at Hamburg.

It must be stressed that the members of the Beatles do not write the history of the books and media. In fact, they themselves have mentioned their friendship with many of Liverpool's black musicians on a number of occasions. By calling them friends we can see the affection that John, Paul, and George had for those that they knew and for their music. The Beatles did not just pick up music from the black community in Liverpool, they hung out there and spent so much time there in those early days that you could almost say they were all living there for a while. John Lennon even mentioned once how they were introduced to cannabis by a Jamaican guy from within the community, which clearly shows they were mixing with people known to them. Some of the Beatles' music shows signs of the things that they picked up, not just from the musicians of Toxteth, but also from many different styles and places. That is what made the Beatles so good: their ability to watch, learn, and adapt something into their own style. They had no problem in talking about this themselves, and much is documented of how they were influenced by black American rhythm and blues performers, Motown artists, Ravi Shankar, and many others. Yet historians keep on failing to document the importance of Liverpool's black musicians in any great detail. I am trying to not make this chapter about the Beatles, however they keep cropping up, and that is because they are so much a part of the history. Liverpool's black musicians did not make the Beatles, and it should never be claimed that they did. However, what they did do was give them friendship and a helping hand, which should never be ignored. The musical talent within the black community was immense and diverse – as it still is today. The Beatles admired it, so it is rather stunning that so little is mentioned about it in their history.

Thankfully, there is a community that will not allow these stories to pass by. Then there are those such as Tony Henry, who pushed the story of Lord Woodbine and Dr James McGrath of the University of Leeds who interviewed many of the performers (some now sadly gone) for his study of the Liverpool 8 musical culture that was submitted towards his PhD. Events continue to be held within the community to recognise the talent of its sons and daughters and a number of future events are in their early stages. These stories refuse to stay buried where sadly some appear to want them to be. The book will surely one day come that will document in detail these amazing performers and all that they did. In my eyes, that is a bestseller waiting to happen.

Ivan Stax, Joey Ankrah, Ramon Sugar Deen, and George Dixon in Joey's studio.

6

Ted 'Kingsize' Taylor

Edward William Taylor was born on 12 November 1939 to Arthur Taylor and Gladys Prescott, with the couple having married in Liverpool in 1933. Edward, or Ted as he was known, was the third of three sons, his brothers being Alan and Arthur. His father, Arthur, was a master bricklayer who had served his apprenticeship for a firm in Formby. At the outbreak of the Second World War, he signed up with the Royal Berkshire regiment for service.

Ted has become used to making headlines throughout the years, with even his birth providing us with a story. On the night of 11 November 1939, Gladys was in her home at No. 3 Vine Grove, Seaforth, with her mother. Tiredness from her pregnancy was affecting her and she told her mother that she was going to try and get herself some rest. As she climbed the stairs her mother followed, and as she did this she spotted her daughter stop and wince in pain. She knew what was happening and quickly pulled her pinny forward and caught the baby as it fell. The clock struck midnight as young Ted entered the world. Everything was fine with both mother and baby, although Ted did receive the nickname 'Midnight' and was called it for a number of years afterwards. His grandmother registered his birth on 14 November and was asked when he was born, to which she replied 'yesterday'. Of course, the 13th was put on his birth certificate, and when Gladys saw it she went along to the registry office and made them write out a new certificate, stating he was born on 12 November. So, if you check the records, that is why Ted has two births registered for himself.

One of Ted's earliest memories concerned the house in Vine Grove. The houses all had iron foot scrapers outside the front door. Their scraper had somehow come loose and was soon gone. In its place, Ted's grandfather positioned a piece of lead piping; that always stayed with him. He also recalled how every Sunday his mother would insist that everyone went to her mother's house, where they would have a sing-song together. Gladys owned a country lap guitar, which she would play as they sang. It was she who taught Ted to harmonise.

During the war, the family were evacuated to Anglesey. Ted's father spent a lot of time away on service and became a sniper for his regiment, who, coincidentally, were the first Brits to enter Hamburg. Arthur had told his sons of how they had come ashore at the harbour

Taylor family album, featuring a young Ted. (Courtesy of Ted 'Kingsize' Taylor)

and his first glance around at Hamburg showed him a scene of utter devastation from the Allied carpet bombing raids. He also told them of the bomb crater that he and a number of colleges had to shelter in when they were spotted by a German sniper. The marksman was so good that they could not escape from that crater for the next four days. As Arthur told Ted, 'That guy was so good that he could have taken your eye out from three miles away.' Arthur always had a huge respect for the Hamburg people and the German soldiers he encountered.

St Thomas school played host to young Ted in his early days of education before he moved up to the 'big school' at Christ Church, where he became the school captain in his final year. By the age of thirteen, Ted was showing his commitment to work: getting up at 4 a.m. every morning to meet the mail train for WHSmith, before setting up their stall at Seaforth station. He would then deliver on his morning paper round before going to school. Afterwards, he would deliver the evening papers then go and prepare the stall at Seaforth station for the next day. A very busy guy indeed, but Ted has always enjoyed working.

It was seeing Lonnie Donegan on TV that really ignited Ted's interest in music. His mother let him have her guitar, which he stripped, painted, and added ordinary strings too. With C, G, and D learned, he was off and running and able to play almost any skiffle song. He would sit on his front doorstep practising the chords and strumming away to different songs. Other kids would come along with their own guitars and they would learn from one another.

His parents wanted Ted to attend the grammar school like his two brothers but Ted was, by now, more interested in music than education. He took the exams for the school and fluffed them on purpose, even though everyone knew that he was more than capable of passing. Just before he turned fifteen, Ted saw a position available with the Co-op stores for an apprentice butcher. He applied and was taken on. Over the next few years he became a qualified butcher, before going on to become a relief manager, then a manager who worked all over the city. However, we are jumping ahead here, so let us enjoy what came next.

His band-playing career started in a fish and chip shop when a boy named Bobby Thomson asked him if he played the guitar. After Ted had replied that he did, Bobby asked him how many chords he knew. 'Four,' said Ted, to which Bobby replied, 'I know three. Shall we start a group?' As simple as that they had a band. The next few Sunday afternoons saw Bobby's house, in Verdis Street, crowded with anyone who had an instrument and wanted to be in a band. It was George James who teamed up with Ted and Bobby to form a band; they used his surname to call the group the James Boys. The lads started off playing skiffle but were soon reverting to rock 'n' roll. During 1957, they appeared at the Cavern Club – which was strictly jazz or skiffle – and opened up with a Little Richard number. Of course, they were thrown out for it. Little Richard, Chuck Berry, Carl Perkins and Fats Domino were exciting, and influenced Ted and the band to play.

In early 1958, the James Boys played a gig alongside the Dominoes, who were so impressed by Ted that they offered him a place in their band, which he accepted. The band now consisted of Ted (lead guitar and vocals), Arthur Baker (vocals), George Watson (guitar/vocals), Charlie Flynn (bass/vocals), Sam Hardie (piano), and Cliff Roberts (drums). They found a number of gigs and even recorded an acetate album at the Lambda studios in Crosby. As with all bands, members changed: Arthur left and George joined the Black Hawks, while Charlie received his call-up papers for national service. In the summer of 1958, Bobby Thomson switched to bass and came in to form a foursome with Ted, Sam and Cliff. This is how the band would stay for the next year as they played their rock 'n' roll and built up a following.

None of the guys had girlfriends when they had first started in the band. However, by 1958 most of them had regular girlfriends who would travel with them when they performed, so there was none of this trying to pull a girl at the gigs. Their gang of friends and fans still supported the band at the clubs, but their girlfriends were now the priority. By 1959, Ted had become engaged to Yvonne Webster, a beautiful blonde girl who he had met at Southport open-air baths. The couple were very happy and had begun making plans for a future marriage.

Ted was a big fan of *The Huckleberry Hound Show* and would tune in to watch whenever it was on. During one episode, the uncle of Huckleberry Hound sent him a crate that contained a kangaroo. Having never seen a kangaroo before, Huckleberry had no idea what it was and called it a king-sized mouse. Brian Kelly, who ran the Lathom Hall and the Jive Hive, was also a fan of the cartoon show and when Brian saw Ted at his next gig he called out 'here comes kingsize Taylor' and both guys laughed. Of course, with Ted being very tall – 6 feet 5 – 'Kingsize' suited him, and the name stuck.

The next change to the band came in October 1959 when Sam Hardie left to take up his police cadet training. Geoff Bethell would stand in with the guys from time to time on piano. They also added another member in the shape of John Kennedy, who also sang, thus giving them Ted, Bobby, and John on vocals.

As the bands popularity grew, the gigs were building. They were now being booked for the bigger venues such as the Aintree Institute, where they went down a treat. Of course, the Institute had the bonus of having the Black Bull pub very close by and this is where the guys would hang out before shows. Changes were aplenty from the summer of 1960, with Charlie Flynn returning to the band on guitar after serving his national service. The band also extended their name to Kingsize Taylor and the Dominoes. They were now up there competing with the top local bands, and as they moved into 1961 another change was about to occur. Priscilla Maria Veronica White, or as we best know her, Cilla Black, joined the band as a feature singer in early 1961 and would get up to sing a few songs during their gigs. Adverts from the day show the band named as Kingsize Taylor and the Dominoes with Swinging Cilla.

It is widely reported in books, newspaper articles, and across the internet that Cilla was the girlfriend of Ted. However, that story is wrong, but Ted knows how it originated:

> The story started after Cilla had become famous. It first appeared in a supplement about Cilla in the Daily Mirror newspaper. She had been asked about her early singing days and had responded that she loved her time with Kingsize Taylor. Of course, being a newspaper it was twisted and was written as the love of her life was Kingsize Taylor. Cilla was just saying that she loved performing with the Dominoes, but as newspapers do, they twisted it.

The music scene in Merseyside was now booming and in full flow. The Dominoes were by now a major player and were mixing it with the best of them. However, an argument over a fee split the band, with Charlie, Cliff, and Geoff leaving the group to join Ian and the Zodiacs. Ted, Bobby and Cilla remained as the Dominoes, while John Kennedy decided he would finish his printing apprenticeship. Dave Lovejoy was brought in on drums, while the Lancashire constabulary lost out when Sam Hardie decided to return to music and rejoin the band.

The band took the changes in their stride and continued to blow people away with their thrilling performances. They had a truly distinctive and powerful voice with Ted, alongside talented musicians. They were up there with the best of the bands and were highly sought after by promoters. The band was rocking the major venues, such as, among others, the Aintree Institue, Orrell Park Ballroom, Jive Hive,

Lathom Hall, and the Cavern Club. However, it was at the Iron Door Club that they were really able to unleash some thumping rock 'n' roll.

Promoter Sam Leach had the foresight to see what the public wanted, and booked the Iron Door Club for a number of all-night sessions. On 6 March 1961, the Dominoes performed alongside the top local bands: the Big Three, the Beatles, the Hurricanes, the Pacemakers, and the Seniors. It was a great success. The crowds were blown away and Sam was quick to follow it up with a larger all-nighter five days later, which saw the same lineup being joined by the Remo Four, the Del Renas, the Pressmen, the Jets, the Jaywalkers, and Faron and the Tempest Tornadoes. The Easter weekend of 1961 saw two more Iron Door all-night gigs for the Dominoes, who were by now also being booked by Geoff Hogarth to play at the club on a regular basis.

In Ted's own words about the Iron Door Club: 'It was just unbelievable, the atmosphere in there. There was no air down there but it was very exciting.' From November 1961, Sam Leach began to put on the Operation Big Beat concerts at the New Brighton Tower Ballroom, of which the Dominoes were major players.

John Frankland had joined the band on guitar and vocals during the summer of '61 to enhance the group, who were by now firmly cemented among the elite bands of Merseyside. They rocked and thumped their way into 1962 before a major player left the band for a short period. Lou Walters, bass player and second singer with Rory Storm and the Hurricanes, had left the band to join the Seniors as they played down in London. The Hurricanes were offered a tour of US army bases and France and needed a suitable replacement. Bobby Thomson fitted the bill and they approached him with an offer. Bobby agreed to do the tour before returning to the Dominoes, then teamed up with the Hurricanes in March 1962. The Dominoes brought in Ken Shalliker on bass as a replacement for Bobby.

The Dominoes continued to impress across Merseyside and the surrounding areas. Bobby Thomson returned from France and extended his stay with the Hurricanes as they took up their summer season at Butlins in Skegness. The Dominoes were booked to perform at the Star-Club in Hamburg during that summer and, as Bobby was not returning until the end of August, they went without him. Cilla chose to stay in Liverpool, though it is unlikely her father would have let her go anyway. While in Hamburg, Ted met Marga Bierfreud, who was a fan of the band at the Star-Club. They became very close and when he returned to Liverpool he promised her he would keep in touch.

Germany had been a thrill for the band, who had loved their time there. The fans and the club loved them as well, and they were invited back for a three-month stint in September. However, they had one problem in Dave Lovelady, who was still studying architecture and unable to go out to Hamburg for so long, thus leaving them needing to find a drummer.

The band's popularity along with the chance of fame had stepped in and caused a divide in the relationship between Ted and Yvonne. Their gig at the Star-Club had basically finally finished it for the couple, who went their own ways. Sadly, it was never to be – fate or stupidity, who knows. However, Ted and Yvonne remain good friends today.

Bobby Thomson informed the band that Ringo Starr was looking to depart from the Hurricanes and that he had told him about the vacancy with the Dominoes, which Ringo was keen to take. He may have been keen but Ted was not, and he was glad when the deal fell through and Ringo joined the Beatles. Ted did not dislike Ringo, he just thought his drumming would not suit the Dominoes. When Bobby returned they prepared for the Star-Club with Brian Redman on drums. During one gig in Liverpool, they played alongside the Hurricanes, who now had sixteen-year-old Gibson Kemp on drums. Ted and Bobby were both in agreement that this was the drummer they wanted in their band, but for now they would have to do without him.

Kingsize Taylor and the Dominoes at the Star-Club, Hamburg. (Courtesy of Ted 'Kingsize' Taylor)

Hamburg was a great success and the crowds flocked to see the band, who were playing to a full house every night. The Beatles appeared at the club in late 1962, and in December that year they were recorded on a four-track portable tape recorder that belonged to Ted. This was not a commercial recording; it was just what happened to have been left on the tape. The bands would use it to listen to their sets. The Beatles were the last band taped. Ted had met a lady in Hamburg named Brigitta Duhnfarth, who came over to stay in Liverpool. She and Ted were married in early 1963 before he returned to Hamburg with the band. Marga was a bit put-out by this news, though she never forgot the Liverpool lad who she had been so taken with.

During December 1962, Ted was being introduced to Brian Epstein at a restaurant in Hamburg called the Flunder. Ted looked a Brian and said, 'who is he?' and carried on with his meal. To Ted, Brian was the guy who sold records in NEMS back in Liverpool. He knew that he was now involved with the Beatles, though he had no interest in him. Brian was a bit put out by Ted's comment, and as Ted was soon to find out he took things like that rather personally.

Ted returned to Liverpool on 4 January 1963. The guys had a few days off before starting a three-month tour of universities across the UK. The tour started around 10/11 January, with the band having to drive through thick snow across the Pennines to make it to the gig at the University of Sheffield. When they arrived, they were informed that they were not commissioned to play. Ted then showed them the contract, but they refused to allow them in. The next night they drove to Manchester, where the same thing happened again. Wondering what was going on, they began to make enquiries and discovered that Brian Epstein had bought out the tour and removed them from it. So, Ted rang Manfred Weissleder and told him the story and of how upset everyone was. Manfred offered them a residency at the Star-Club beginning in March 1963, which they accepted.

Before taking up their residency, the Dominoes approached Gibson Kemp about joining them. He was up for it and began to gig with the band. Being only seventeen, he had to apply for a permit to work abroad. Once it was obtained, he was free to go off to the Star-Club. The band was given a large flat to live in on the Große Freiheit, close to the club. They were also protected as they worked for Manfred Weissleder, so, as with the other Star-Club bands, they were unlikely to come up against any trouble in the area. They were local stars and as Ted put it, 'I was treated like royalty the whole time I was at

Chubby Checker and the Dominoes at Hamburg airport, 1963. The band had played on the runway to welcome Chubby, who was coming to appear at the Star-Club. (Courtesy of Ted 'Kingsize' Taylor)

the Star-Club. What more do you want from life?' He went on, 'The Star-Club had the best back line around and every band would use it. You would not be able to afford the equipment that was on that stage. It was the best of everything there, best drum kit, Hammond organ. Steinway piano, the best fender guitars. A performer wanted for nothing'.

Hamburg became home to the band, who continued to pack out the club and thrill an audience. They would also play dates at the other Star-Clubs in various German cities. Their popularity was growing and it was not going unnoticed. Decca offered the band a contract to record in Germany, which they accepted and cut a few tracks. They also recorded for the Philips and Ariola labels. In August 1963, Howie Casey joined the band on saxophone. They recorded a live album for Ariola at the Star-Club, before an offer was put to them that would forever confuse researchers of the band's recordings. The band played with some of the biggest names in the business at the Star-Club, including Little Richard, Jerry Lee Lewis, Fats Domino, Johnny Kidd, the Everly Brothers, Ray Charles, Joey Dee and the Starliters, Sam the Sham, Bill Haley, Little Eva, and on, and on.

Ted gave an insight into a day in the life of a Star-Club musician:

The worst scenario would be that there was only three bands playing at the Star-Club and you start in the week at 6:00. You're then gonna be on at 9 pm, 12 am, and 3 am. You have nowhere to go because in two hours time you have got to be back on the stage. So, it's straight into Gretel and Alfons, a meal in the Mambo, or somewhere else close by as you needed to be somewhere within walking distance of the club for your sets. So you stay there and you play. So, for around ten hours you are confined to the area around the Star-Club. After your final set, it was likely to be a wind-down in Gretel and Alfons till around 7 am before heading to bed. When you are all up and awake it would be rehearsal time before heading into town and maybe looking at the instruments in Steinways store. You would then return to the St Pauli area and start the process all over again. Every weekend, the Star-Club would be open for twelve hours and whether you set finished at 2 am or 6 am, everyone did the same thing and went down to the Fischmarkt [fish market]. That was the place to be.

The band was approached by a guy one night who asked them whether they were under any type of contract. They explained that they had a contract and he replied, 'Well, would you like to record an album under a different name and we will give you £1,000.' The guys agreed on the spot – after all, it was a lot of money. After one performance at the club, which finished at around 1 a.m., the band made their way to the Rayell studio to record the album. They did every song live and in one take and were paid their money. Of course, being under contract they had to use a false name; they came up with three ideas: Noddy and the Red Toecaps, Boots Wellington and his Rubber Band, and the Shakers. Thankfully they chose the latter, and the album entitled *Let's do the Twist, Locomotion, Slop, Hully Gully, Monkey* was released in Germany at the end of 1963 on the Polydor label. A number of singles came from the album, which were also released under the name of the Shakers. 'Hippy Hippy Shake'/'Money' was brought out in Germany in September 1963, while 'Hippy Hippy Shake'/'Dr Feelgood' made its UK release in November of the same year. Later in February 1964, 'Whole Lotta Lovin'/'I Can Tell' was released in both Germany and the UK.

During 1963 the band had been hired to back Audrey Arno on her single 'Bitte Bleib Doch Bei Mir' (Please Stay With Me). They had backed her a number of times at the Star-Club so were happy to oblige. On the day of the recording session, Audrey was given the devastating news that her father had passed away. The guys were stunned when she announced that she wanted to finish the recording and had nothing but admiration for her. Steve Aldo teamed up with the band for a couple of months in late 1963, before departing in November. Another member leaving was Sam Hardie, who went to play with Tony Sheridan. Dave Woods came in as a second sax player and, not long after, they were joined by a third saxophonist in the shape of Muhammad Hari, a Moroccan Frenchman.

Ted also spoke of his admiration for the Star-Club and Manfred Weissleder:

> I never went to any other clubs in the area as there was no need too. The atmosphere in the Star-Club was electric and you really were part of a big family. Manfred was a lovely man. I once walked into the club and he was sitting there wearing a new leather jacket. I told him that I liked it and he made me try it on before saying 'it fits you, keep it' Horst Fascher's mother would wash all our shirts for us. I mean, what other club ever treated its performers that way instead of as a commodity?

In 1963, they appeared on the album *Liverpool Beat – Star-Club*, which was recorded live at the club in Hamburg. They shared the album with the Bobby Patrick Big Six, with the Dominoes taking the A-side of the album. During 1964, the band again appeared alongside the Bobby Patrick Big Six for the live Star-Club album *Twist Time I'm Star-Club Hamburg 2*.

It is almost impossible to keep up with what the band recorded and under what name they did it. They were involved in all kinds of recordings. They had put down another album only for Ted's voice to be dubbed over by a German singer named Hans Werner. Ted later recorded two duets with Hans that came out in Germany. They were the band that Alex Harvey had on his album *Alex Harvey and His Soul Band*, released in Germany in 1964.

A number of singles were brought out as Kingsize Taylor and the Dominoes, including 'The Fortune Teller'/'Never In a Hundred Years' in Germany, November 1963; 'Memphis Tennessee'/'Money' in the UK in 1963; 'Memphis Tennessee'/'Dizzy Miss Lizzy' in Germany in 1964; 'Sky Boat Song'/'Down In The Valley' in Germany in 1964; and the Teenbeat EP in the UK in 1964, which featured four songs from the Live Star-Club album *All Around The World*: 'Slippin and Slidin', 'You Can't Sit Down', and 'Hello Josephine'.

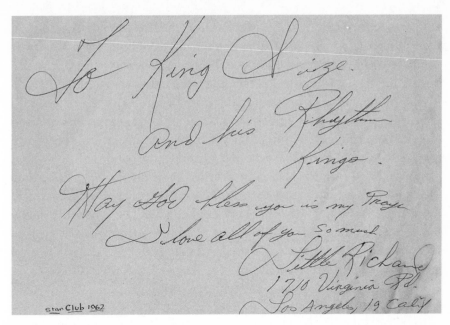

Little Richard's signed note to Ted Taylor, which includes his USA address. (Courtesy of Ted 'Kingsize' Taylor)

It was the Decca single 'Stupidity'/'Bad Boy' that really took off for the band and gave them a No. 1 chart position in Germany. The guys travelled over for promotion reasons when the single was released in the UK. They appeared on the popular TV show *Thank Your Lucky Stars* and on the 'Saturday Club, Radio Show' on 9 May 1964. That same day, the Dominoes began backing Chuck Berry on his first ever UK tour, appearing in their home town on 17 May at the Liverpool Odeon. Carl Perkins, Gene Vincent, the Animals, and the Swinging Blue Jeans were also part of this tour, which ended on 31 May.

On 24 July the band appeared on the TV show *Ready Steady Go!* performing 'Somebody's Always Trying'. Alongside them on the show were the Rolling Stones, the Animals, Sandie Shaw, the Fourmost, the Mojos, and the Paramounts. The tour had been a fantastic thrill and the band took up a number of engagements around the UK. However, Ted was longing to return to Hamburg, which became a problem to the other band members who had grown accustomed to being back home. They wanted to stay and work in Britain and these differences led to Ted leaving the band.

It remains a crying shame that this band never found the fame that they fully deserved. Ted had one of the most distinctive and powerful voices ever to come out of Merseyside, the UK, or anywhere else. Every member of the band was a talent in their own right and most went on to find success within the industry. Being based in Germany during the rush to sign the Merseyside bands had left them unexposed to the managers and producers back in Britain. However, the guys were stars in Germany and I doubt any of them, given the chance, would have changed a thing. They left us with plenty of recordings and memories and remain respected for the great band that they were.

Ted went to London where he worked on a few tracks at the New Olympic Studios with the guitarist Jimmy Page, who would later find fame with the Yardbirds and Led Zeppelin. In late 1964 the single 'Somebody's Always Trying'/'Looking For My Baby' was released by Decca under the name King Size Taylor. It featured Jimmy Page on guitar and Clem Cattini on drums. Ted had also recorded 'I'm Hangin' Up My Heart For You' in a Manchester studio around 1963/64, and this track was later released on the King Size Taylor EP.

In December of '64, Brigitta gave birth to their son, who they named Mark. Ted returned to Hamburg with the Mersey 5 as the New Dominoes in 1965. He later teamed up with the Griff Parry Five before recruiting a number of musicians to form Kingsize Taylor and His Band. On Valentine's Day 1965, Ted was at the Star-Club with Brigitta and little Mark when Manfred Weissleder decided that he would show the child off to the audience. He took Mark on stage and introduced him to the crowd, thus making Mark the youngest person ever to appear on the famous stage. The gigs still went well and the bookings still came in, but by the end of 1966 the fun had all gone out of it for Ted. He was, by now, fed up with what the music industry had become and called it a day. Polydor released the King Size Taylor single 'Thinkin''/'Let Me Love You' in the UK in 1967.

Ted returned to his mother's home in Crosby, Liverpool. One day while feeling nostalgic he went to visit his old house in Vine Grove, only to discover that it had been demolished. Standing in the street outside where the house had once stood, he noticed the piece of lead piping that his grandfather had once put into the pavement in place of the foot scraper, but that was all that remained. He began to look for work and found a position as a butcher in Southport. Being a person who hates to commute, he decided to buy a house in the town. Within a few years Ted had bought his own shop and was making a decent living from being a butcher. His marriage to Brigitta ended in 1969, and he later married Barbara O'Neil in spring 1973 in Southport. Ted

Ted Taylor and Carol Elvin on the balcony of the Dominoes' flat in the Große Freiheit. (Courtesy of Ted 'Kingsize' Taylor)

became known locally as a meat artist. He was so creative with meat that if you were throwing a dinner party you could order from him and he would create you something that, placed on your table, would stun the guests and have people taking photographs of it.

The offers kept coming in for Ted to perform again but he had no interest at all. During the 1970s he relocated the reel tape recording he had made of the Beatles at the Star-Club in 1962, and so began a lengthy court battle to have it released – which, in 1977, it eventually was. In fact, it would be over twenty years before Ted had anything to do with music again, and even that only came about as he was helping out a local charity. It was during 1999 that he agreed to help out the Merseycats charity when they approached him after the number of '60s musicians helping them out had dropped to an alarming level. At first, he was not keen to do it, but he took it on and would jam with whatever musicians were on stage during the Thursday night events.

In 2002, Ted played at the 40th anniversary celebrations of the Star-Club in Hamburg. There had been people uncertain that the event held at the Kaiserkeller would not be a success. However, all those thoughts were blown away when an estimated half a million people attend over the celebrations weekend. The Große Freiheit was jam-packed and the musicians were stopped everywhere they went for autographs and photographs – a clear sign of the high esteem that the club and musicians were held in.

While there he met up with Marga Bierfreund again; they were both delighted to see each other. Forty years apart had changed nothing about how each cared about the other, and this time they remained in contact. They were clearly besotted and in love, and it soon led to the ringing of wedding bells. Ted and Marga married at St John's Church in Birkdale on 17 May 2003. They remained in the area and Marga helped Ted to run the butcher business.

Ted and Marga, along with Wes Paul, began a venture to raise money to help '60s musicians who had become ill or fallen on hard times. From 13 November 2005, they put shows on at the Cavern Club every Sunday, which featured many of the biggest names from the Merseybeat era alongside up and coming bands. 'Sound Of The Sixties' ran until 2 September 2007 and raised thousands of pounds to help those in need. Ted and Wes would perform and Marga would give a song. Many of the legends giving their time to the events included, among others, the Undertakers, the Del Renas, the Mojo's, the Jaywalkers, the Zodiacs, Faron's Flamingos, the Clayton Squares, Karl Terry, and, of course, the Dominoes.

Ted and Marga decided to move to Hamburg in 2006 and held an emotional farewell gig on 20 August at the Cavern Club. Of course, they used the event to raise money for charity. With accommodation,

Karl Terry, John Frankland, Ted Taylor, and John Kennedy outside 'Taylor's Bar', Ted's former butcher shop in Birkdale.

removals, and all arrangements sorted and in place, the couple said their goodbyes to Liverpool and headed into a warm welcome in Hamburg.

Ted began to play in Hamburg with his band Kingsize Taylor and the Brotherhood of Rock and Soul. In 2008, they released a CD album titled *Kingsize Taylor and Brotherhood Of Rock 'N' Soul*, which had been recorded at the High Gain studio in Hamburg. Alongside Ted on the album were Chris Thornton and Volker Schlag on guitar, Thorsten Rejzek on bass, Nick Oosterhuis on organ/piano, Ecki Hofmann on saxophone, and Björn Hofmann on drums.

The first Friday of every month was always the day that people from the Star-Club family would meet up at Kemp's Bar, which is run by Tina and Gibson Kemp. This clearly shows the affection that was held not only for the Star-Club but also for those who performed, worked, and attended the venue and created the history that they did.

Sadly, in early 2016, Ted's world was shattered when his beloved Marga passed away in Hamburg. The couple have a love story second to none. The way that they found each other after forty years apart and fell in love all over again is nothing short of remarkable – and rather special.

By late 2016 Ted had returned to live in Southport, though the music has not left him and he continues to enjoy doing what he does best. The Dominoes have played farewell gigs in Hamburg and Liverpool, where they have thrilled and rocked audiences – who still flock to see them perform. Let us hope there is another farewell gig still to come.

Ted has become a regular performer at the anniversary shows at home and abroad for places such as the Kaiserkeller, Star-Club, Lathom Hall, Cavern Club, and many more. He continues to perform in public and contributes to a number of musical charities. He is a guy who suffers no fools and says things as they are. Ted is also a staunch believer in giving credit to the people who deserve it, especially in relation to the roots of the Merseybeat scene. Ted is also a very generous man with a heart as big as himself. He is a musical legend, an icon of rock 'n' roll, who has been there and done it with the best of them. However, there is no 'big I am' with him. He is very approachable and treats everyone in his company as a friend. That smile and friendliness are still there in Ted – and the voice, oh! That wonderful voice is still belting out those songs.

Mark Taylor said of his dad, Ted:

My earliest recollection of hearing dad sing was when at the age of around nine I was flicking through my mother's record collection of mainly mainstream rock n roll from the sixties and the world cup Argentina theme tune when I stumbled across a gem. It was Kingsize Taylor and the Dominoes with a tune called 'Stupidity' on an acetate record. Only one side had a track on it, while the other was completely shiny and smooth. So I stuck it on the turntable and it hit me like a hammer. I was into the Bay City Rollers at this time and the music on this record was certainly nothing like them. My early childhood was complicated and it was a while before one of my childhood dreams came true. I was the frontman of a band on the same bill as my dad and there he was banging out 'Stupidity' like it was on the record. A surreal moment for me that I will always treasure. Obviously, with the aid of the internet, Ted's back catalogue has become freely available to all, including myself, and this has allowed me to do a lot of catching up on what I can only describe as 'the business'. Kingsize was a front runner for Merseybeat and Hamburg Beat and should – and will – go down in the history books as the man that taught the Beatles – and his son – how to rock 'n' roll.

Ted and Mark Taylor. (Courtesy of David Conlin)

7

Some Other Guys and Girls

The Dennisons

In 1961, a few friends decided to try their hands at the music mania that was gaining so much popularity around the Merseyside area. They called themselves the Dennisons and are believed to have taken the name from a Liverpool street. If this is true, then it is very possible that they took it from Denison Street, which was located off Dock Road, just outside of the city centre at the start of the Vauxhall area. This street is well known for being the home of Kitty Wilkinson, the 'Saint of the Slums', who opened up her home as a wash house during the cholera epidemic of 1832, thus saving many local lives. History lesson over, now back to the band, which consisted of Eddie Parry (vocals), Steve McLaren (lead guitar), Ray Scragge (rhythm guitar), Alan Willis (bass) and Clive Hornby (drums).

The guys had first started off by following around a band called the Ravens and learning their chords. Once they were happy with their sound they began to look for gigs, with Hornby's father managing their bookings. They were signed up very quickly by the MICC club in Melling to a contract of forty Friday night performances. This was fantastic for a new band deal and gave them regular work. Some bands just have that certain something, and the Dennisons were certainly in that category. They had it all: looks, style, musical ability, and performance. The word spread fast about this exciting new band and their following grew, with club owners and promoters eager to book them. They became regulars at the popular venues across Merseyside and made their Cavern Club debut in May 1962. For a new band, their rapid rise into the pool of top local groups was very impressive. It was also fully deserved as they were a seriously good act.

Their fan base rose so much that a fan club was started for them in the summer of 1962. Mary Travis, of Vincent Road in Litherland, started and ran the club. Of course, their success was not going without notice further afield either. The guys decided to turn professional, though Alan Willis was not keen to leave his apprenticeship and decided to leave the band. Terry Carson replaced him on bass and the band remained popular. The impact that these boys were making brought the interest from the record companies and by 1963 they had signed a contract with Decca. They had also signed a management deal with Manchester-based Kennedy Street Enterprises. The Dennisons were by now being tipped for big things. Their debut single 'Be My Girl' was self-composed and is alleged to have been written in the dressing room of the Cavern Club. It was released in July 1963 with 'Little Latin Lupe Lu' as the B-side. The song made it to No. 46 on the hit parade. Tours of the UK followed with some of the biggest names around, including the Walker Brothers, Dave Clark Five, Dusty Springfield, Dionne Warwick, and the Yardbirds. They played on a tour of Scotland with Ben E .King too, who was so impressed by the band that he wrote them a song that they later recorded. They were placed third in the 1963 *Mersey Beat* poll results, with only the Beatles and Gerry and the Pacemakers coming ahead of them. That is some achievement and clearly shows the size of their local fan base.

Their second single 'Walking The Dog'/'You Don't Know What Love Is' was released in April 1964 and made it to No. 36 in the charts. The band appeared and sang this single on the TV music show *Ready, Steady, Go!* on 22 May. The Beatles offered the band their song 'All My Loving' to record, though the Dennisons turned it down. They had their own reasons and there is very little point in claiming – as some do – that this was their downfall. They were their own band, and fair play to them for doing things the way that they chose. 'Nobody Like My Babe'/'Lucy (You Sure Did It This Time)' became their third Decca single. The song failed to chart but, as with their other recordings, it was far better than its final position indicated. Eddie Parry left the band in 1965 and was replaced by Colin Areety. By 1966 the band had split and went their separate ways. Clive Hornby took up acting and went on to play Jack Sugden in *Emmerdale*. In 1991, Terry Carson passed away and the band reformed for a tribute concert in his honour. Eddie Parry was to pass away in 1995. The remaining band members came together for Clive Hornby's appearance on *This Is Your Life* in 1997. Gerry Marsden and Ken Dodd also sent him messages during the episode. Sadly Ray Scragg (2001), Steve McLaren (2007), and Clive Hornby (2008) have all since passed away. Their singles for Decca, along with their live Cavern Club recordings of 'Devoted To You' and 'You Better Move On', remain to remind us of just how much talent that these guys had.

Rita Hughes

Rita was born in Chester in 1946. She lived in Broughton with her parents, who were publicans – and maybe it was the pub environment where she learnt to sing. And, boy, could this young lady sing! In 1962, at the age of just sixteen, she joined a local band named the Pacemakers. The band had to change their name when Brian Epstein heard about them due to him managing Gerry and the Pacemakers. They changed their name to the rather clever Four Hits and a Miss. The band consisted of Rita (vocals), Davis Jones (lead guitar), Geoff Dawson (rhythm guitar), Owen Ricketts (bass), and George Roberts (drums). Terry Lynch was soon to take over drumming duties from George, who left the band. They started off with a number of local gigs and went down a storm. Very quickly they became the most sought-after band in Chester and offers from outside the area soon followed. Liverpool promoters began to hear about this popular band and were soon booking them to play at their venues.

Although a band from outside of Merseyside, they played enough times within the area to be included in this book. A number of their gigs were at the Cavern Club, and the band have their name on one of the bricks that make up the Cavern wall of fame. The groups appeal soon caught the attention of a number of record companies. They chose to sign with Pye Records, who contracted them to record on the Piccadilly label. This period also included a name change: Rita became known as 'Jeannie', and the band as Jeannie and the Big Guys. Their first single was released in October 1963, a wonderful version of 'Don't Lie To Me' with the B-side being 'Boys'. This was followed in February 1964 by a second single 'I Want You'/'Sticks And Stones'. Sadly, neither charted, but both were very decent recordings that had the potential to make the hit parade.

David Jones left to join the Peter Dee Band and was replaced on lead guitar by Peter Johnson. Phil Blackwell was brought in on keyboards as the band looked to advance their playing style. Both Peter and Phil had been part of the Exchequers before they joined the

Jeannie and Big Guys. (Courtesy of Owen Rickets)

group. However, Rita (Jeannie) saw her future elsewhere and by the end of 1964 she had parted company with the band. They continued as the Big Guys, with Owen Rickets later going on to play with the Toplins for a short period,

Rita fronted the band Earl Royce and the Olympics, before pursuing a solo career. She was soon signed up to EMI and recorded under the name of 'Cindy Cole'. Her first solo single, 'A Love Like Yours'/'He's Sure The Boy I Love', came out on the Columbia label in March 1965. Oddly, she next recorded under the name of 'Jeannie' under Parlophone, releasing the single 'I Love Him'/'With Any Other Girl' in October 1965. It was then back to Columbia records in July 1966 for her third solo single 'Lonely City Blue Boy' with 'Just Being Your Baby (Turns Me On)' as the B-side. None of the songs charted but, once again, they were of a high standard. Rita continued her solo career, eventually moving into the cabaret scene, where she was very successful. Sadly, in 1988, Rita passed away. She is still missed by her family and friends and is remembered fondly for her wonderful voice.

Tony Goldby

Anthony Archibald Golby was born on 5 January 1945 to Nancy and Archie Golby at Stanley hospital in the Kirkdale area of Liverpool. He was a pupil at Saint Francis De Sales School, and after having begged his parents for a guitar Tony was delighted to receive one on Christmas Day in 1958. The *Skiffle Rock Tutor* book set him on his way, though he was finding it too difficult to press down the chords. Dave Swan offered to help him but told him the action was too high on his guitar and could not be adjusted. Basically, the gap between the strings and fingerboard was too big. This was why Tony could not hold down the chords but when Dave allowed him to use his guitar he could form them pretty fine. After a few lessons, his father bought Tony a Broadway electric guitar for £25 and a small Selmer amp called 'The Little Giant' and he was off and running.

The lessons continued and soon he had teamed up with another guitarist: Dennis Conroy. They practised together before deciding to form a group in 1960. Alan Walton came in on drums and the band gave themselves the name of the Premiers – after his drum kit. Their first paid gig was in Birkenhead, where they received 7s 6d each for their performance. Tony's father did a lot of work for Jack Yue (the king of Chinatown) and managed to get the lads a few gigs at the 21 Club in Berry Street.

They played songs along the lines of 'Travelling Light', 'Livin Doll', 'When The Girl In Your Arms', and 'Girl Of My Dreams'. However, their musical direction was about to change. They heard about a band that was playing at the Cavern Club. None of them had ever been to the club, but they opted to go along and see what all the fuss was about. They were stunned when the Beatles came on stage jumping and fooling around and playing songs that they had never heard before. From then on they would go and watch the Beatles as often as possible and pick up tips to try out themselves.

Tony took an apprenticeship as an engineer with Essex Partners in Bridgewater Street. In August 1962, he heard that the Beatles were going to be filmed at the Cavern for a TV show. He had to be there and worked out a plan to do it. His lunch break was between 12 and 1 p.m, and running to the Cavern from his workplace took ten minutes, which left him forty minutes to see the Beatles getting filmed. On Wednesday 22 August, Tony ran to the Cavern with his butties to eat. However, the Beatles were nowhere to be seen. A camera was positioned in the main archway but nothing was happening. Tony was anxious to get back to work but as time passed by he found himself with a decision to make: a job or the Beatles? At 1 p.m. he decided he should stay as his job was probably gone. The Beatles came on stage around 2 p.m. Tony recalled, 'A thunderous shouting of "We Want Pete" went on for quite a while.' It was just one week since Pete Best had been sacked and fans were still angry. For Tony, Pete had been the Beatle who had stuck out the most, so the anger felt justified. He continued, 'The Beatles burst into "Some Other Guy" and everyone was bopping along' – on the TV recording, you can hear someone shout 'We want Pete' as the song ends. The Beatles played the song twice for filming. Tony remembered George breaking a string and Paul saying 'fancy breaking a string on telly'. Tony has never forgotten the day he was present at such an event. He left the club at 4 p.m. and ran to work. The foreman, Harry Gardner, threatened him with the sack. Tony apologised and promised never to do it again.

The Beatles went on to have a trail of No. 1 singles, and the impression they left on Tony remained. Ronnie Dodd replaced Alan on drums in late 1963, with Lofthouse in on bass. The band now looked to create a new sound. Tony walked into Frank Hessey's music shop and noticed three new Rickenbacker guitars hanging up. He ran home to tell his father, who returned to the shop with him to see. His dad paid £146 for the same Rickenbacker that John Lennon was using and Tony paid him back 10s a week. As Tony pointed out: 'John Lennon was the only person who had one back them so I was probably the second person in Liverpool to own one and possibly the UK.' The Premiers continued to play until 1965, when they split and went their own ways. Tony later played bass with Shuffler Sound and Stateside Review before forming the duo Grapevine with Ivan Stax.

Irene Green (Tiffany)

Irene started her career when she successfully answered an advert for an audition to be the singer of the all-girl band the Liverbirds. The girls toured around the country before Irene left to go solo. After performing locally she teamed up with the Four Dimensions in April 1964 and they gigged under the name of Tiffany's Dimensions. Despite being a band,

Tiffany would still sing solo at times and the lads would also play as a group by themselves. They went on tour and were being hotly tipped for success. In October 1964, they were performing at Glasgow when all of their instruments were stolen. Everything was on HP, so they still had to pay it all off. They scraped around to borrow equipment and carried on, and you have to wonder if this setback cost them future success.

Tiffany left the band in early 1965 and caught the eye of producers. In July of that year she released the single 'Am I Dreaming' on Parlophone, B-sided with 'I Know'. These are two fantastic recordings and the single should really have charted. She also appeared in the short TV film *Liverpool a Go-go*, presented by Bob Wooler. She can be seen in the film singing 'Reelin and a Rockin' and 'I Know' on top of an open-top bus. In April 1966, she released a second single, backed by Liverpool band the Thoughts. The single 'Find Out What's Happening' was released by Parlophone, with the B-side 'Baby Don't Look Down'. Once more, these are two great recordings, though the public failed to latch on and it never charted. The record label ended their contract and, as far as can be found, Tiffany never recorded again. It is shocking that this very talented lady never found the success that she deserved.

The Del Renas

A band was formed in 1958 that included Ray Walker on guitar and vocals, Brian Young on bass, Brian James on piano and clavioline, and Brian Dean on drums. The band's name is believed to have been taken from a local shipping line, however a search of the shipping line index reveals no company of any similar name. In 1956, the Pacific Steam Navigation Co. (PSNC) launched the latest cruise ship, the *Reina Del Mar*, with the ship making her maiden voyage from Liverpool on 3 May. She became a regular Liverpool-based ship that took tourists to many destinations across the world. It is possible – and indeed very likely – that this ship is which the band was named after. By the start of 1959, the band had recruited two new members: Terry Fisher joined on lead guitar and Derek Green came in on rhythm guitar. With Ray on vocals, they were often billed as Ray and the Del Renas. The band also played a number of instrumental numbers – and they did them well. They became a very decent band who would mix it with the big groups at the popular venues. Bob Wooler was so impressed by the band when he heard them play that he gave them forty-two advanced bookings at the Cavern Club.

That is more than he ever gave the Beatles at any one time. With Brian James using a Clavoline, they were one of the first local bands to use the electric keyboard. By early 1960 they had brought in Joan Molloy to front the band as a singer. By the end of that year Joan had left, as had Brian Young, who the band replaced on bass with John Withy. They ended the year by playing at the Litherland Town Hall on 27 December alongside the Beatles. This was the night that the Beatles had been billed as 'Live From Hamburg' and stunned everyone with their improvement.

The Del Renas continued to play and entertain crowds, but by 1962 the band was once more losing members as both Ray Walker and Brian Dean departed. Ian Howe became their new drummer as the band set about changing their style to bring a number of rock 'n' roll and rhythm and blues songs into their set. They remained just as popular under this new style and the bookings were plentiful right into 1963. Then, something happened that would once more split and change the band. An offer was presented to them to travel to Germany and play in Hamburg, but some of the band members were reluctant to travel abroad. Green, Fisher, and Howe chose to stay on in Merseyside and formed a new band – the Motifs – who played together until the mid-1960s. The remaining members recruited John Fallon and went to play in Hamburg in March 1963. They returned in May and were booked straight away to record for Oriele for the *This Is Merseybeat* album. The band continued to play the local circuit until splitting up in 1964. The guys have reformed over the years for special events, including the Mathew Street festival.

Mona Best

Alice Mona Shaw was born on 3 January 1924 in Delhi, India, to Thomas and Mary Shaw. Mona was raised and educated in India, where she also later met Donald Peter Scanland, a marine engineer, and a romance began that led to the birth of her first child, Randolph Peter Scanland, who was born in Madras in 1941. Donald was sadly killed while serving during the Second World War. Mona later met John Best, a PT officer serving with the British Army. The couple married on 7 March 1944 at St Thomas' Cathedral in Bombay. In January 1945 a son, Rory, was born to them. Randolph, who had become known by his middle name – Peter – took on John's surname after the marriage, and from then on was known as Pete Best.

With the war over, John wanted to return back to his home city of Liverpool. Mona was in agreement and the family boarded the *Georgic* for the journey to the UK; they docked in Liverpool on Christmas Day 1945. They lived at the Best's family home for a while, before taking a small flat in Cases Street. From here they moved to Princess Drive, before settling in Queenscourt Road in the West Derby area of the city in 1948.

The story goes that in 1954 Mona pawned her jewellery to place a bet on the horse 'Never Say Die' in the Derby, with the horse winning the race a 33/1. She then used her winnings to buy a large Victorian house at No. 8 Hayman's Green, West Derby. Whether the betting story is true or not, the family had moved into their new home by 1957 and history was about to be made.

The house at Hayman's Green had a huge cellar and Mona told Pete and his friends that they could use it if they wanted somewhere to hang out. Then, while watching a TV clip about the 2i's Coffee Bar in London, Mona decided that she could use the basement to open a bar such as this. The idea was that the club – the Casbah – would be for members only and that those members would be friends of Pete or invited by him. The opening night was scheduled for 29 August 1959 with the Les Stewart Quartet booked to perform. However, the band fell out after an argument and cancelled. The gig was taken by the Quarrymen, who featured John Lennon and Paul McCartney. However, before they were accepted, Mona made them help with the decorating of the club.

The Casbah became a huge success and a popular venue for those who wanted to watch live bands. When Pete joined the Beatles in 1960, Mona booked them at the club and promoted them in every way she could. She also booked the Knotty Ash village hall and St John's Hall in Tuebrook and put the band on the bill there. After Pete, Paul, and George had been deported back from Hamburg it was Mona who made constant phone calls to locate their instruments and have them returned to the UK. Along with promoting and booking the Beatles she was also running the Casbah, which was thriving and attracting many of the top local bands. This lady was simply miles ahead of her time.

The Beatles were the last band to play at the club, which closed on 24 June 1962 – just weeks before Mona gave birth to her third son, Vincent Roag Best. Within a few weeks Pete had been sacked by the band and replaced by Ringo Starr. Mona sought out Brian Epstein in search of an answer, though he refused to see her. That was probably a wise decision on Brian's part as she was not a lady to mess with.

The Casbah Club that she started is now a Grade II-listed building and has become a mecca for tourists. Live bands still perform at the club, which remains the most authentic Beatles-related venue in the city. Sadly, Mona passed away on 9 October 1988. Her importance upon the Merseybeat scene should never be underestimated or forgotten.

Faron Ruffley

If you have never heard of Faron Ruffley then where have you been? The guy sticks out like a sore thumb. He was born William Ruffley on 8 January 1942 in Liverpool to William Ruffley and Annie Harley. His father was a musician who could play almost any instrument. He had played with the Ted Heath Band and had once given ukulele lessons to George Formby. Young William, or 'Faron' as he was known, was an out and out eccentric. The name Faron is believed to have derived from a family Cherokee name; whatever the true origins, it stuck, and that is the name that he has since been known by.

Faron had clearly inherited his father's love and ability of music. He began to play instruments with a number of friends and sing on stage when the opportunity arose. He formed a band with friends called the Odd Spots before joining Johnny Tempest and the Tornadoes. Tragically, Johnny Tempest died aged just twenty-one. Faron was asked to become the lead singer of the band, who changed their name to Faron and the Tempest Tornadoes. They did well on the local circuit, where they played all the main venues alongside the popular bands. In mid-1961 Faron had left the band to be replaced by Earl Preston. He was now approached by Gerry and the Pacemakers who asked him to join them for their stint at the Top Ten Club in Hamburg; Faron agreed, and the band went out to perform at the end of July 1961. However, disputes among them saw Faron leave and return to the UK. Once home, he teamed up with Robin and the Ravens as lead singer. The band comprised of Faron, Nicky Crouch (lead guitar), Billy Jones (rhythm guitar), Eric London (bass), and Trevor Morais (drums). They worked well together and successfully set about gigging. They very quickly accepted the suggestion of Cavern DJ Bob Wooler that they should rename the band Faron's Flamingos. Bob had also nicknamed Faron 'the panda-footed prince of prance' due to his onstage antics.

The band did well and quickly established themselves through playing at major venues alongside the most popular bands. They gained a decent following, with many of their fans looking on in awe of the lively – and at times crazy – singer of the band. The Flamingos were beginning to attract the attention of promoters outside of the city as the word spread about their rocking show. In 1962, they were offered and accepted a tour of the US bases in France. However, Eric London was reluctant to travel over and give up his job so he left the band and was replaced by Dave Cooper (known as 'Mushy').

One requirement of the Merseyside bands that toured France was that they brought a female singer with them. The Flamingos took along a lady named Pam Connolly, who was not a singer but managed to do the job well. The tour was from May–June and the band was based at the Evreux-Fauville air base. They are believed to have gone down so well that the base named their club the Flamingo Club. However, their time in France was tinged with problems, which led to Billy Jones leaving the band. During a trip to Paris they met Paddy Chambers in a bar and he agreed to join them. By the time that they returned to the UK, Dave Cooper had left too, with Faron taking over on bass. So, we now had the classic lineup of Nicky Crouch (lead guitar), Paddy Chambers (rhythm guitar), Faron Ruffley (bass and vocals), and Trevor Morais (drums). One sad note was that Pam Connolly, who had toured with the group in France, tragically passed away at a very young age.

This was a seriously good band that thrilled audiences wherever they played. In May 1963, they were invited along to the Rialto Ballroom on Upper Parliament Street in Liverpool to take part in the recording of the album *This Is Merseybeat*. The band recorded four songs that appeared on the two album releases: 'Let's Stomp', 'Talkin About You', 'Shake Sherry', and 'So Fine'. Oriole also signed the band up to produce a couple of singles. The Flamingos recorded an incredibly powerful version of the Contours 'Do You Love Me', though the producers went against the band's wishes and relegated the song to the B-side of the single with 'See If She Cares' becoming the side-A. The single was released at the end of May 1963 but failed to chart, which is hardly surprising as 'Do You Love Me' should have been the A-side. Plus, Oriole was not a big enough label to promote the song. The Flamingos played a short tour with Brian Poole and the Tremeloes and one night, during a performance at the St Helens Plazza, the Tremeloes asked Faron if he would write out the words of the song. He agreed and thought very little of it. The Tremeloes took the song back to their label – Decca – and recorded it. In October 1963, the song went to No. 1, which is where it stayed for three weeks. Listen to both versions

Faron Ruffley. (Courtesy of Mave Atherton)

and decide for yourself whether you think that the Flamingos' version is far superior to that of the Tremeloes.

In October of that year, while the Tremeloes were enjoying a No. 1 success with the Flamingos' idea, Faron and the guys released their second single, 'Shake Sherry'/'Give Me Time'. It was another great recording that sadly failed to make a chart impact. Watching what could have been had hurt the band, and they never recovered from it. By the end of 1963, they had split and gone their separate ways. Nicky Crouch went on to join the Mojo's, releasing a number of charting singles including 'Everything's Alright', 'Why Not Tonight', and 'Seven Daffodils'. Trevor Morais went on to join Rory Storm and the Hurricanes, before co-founding the Peddlers in 1966, who went on to record a number of singles and albums. Trevor left the band in the early 1970s and joined Quantum Jump. He went on to become a top session musician and has performed with many big-named stars as well as running the El Cortijo Studio in Malaga, Spain.

As for Paddy and Faron, they teamed up with Johnny Hutchinson after the Big Three had broken up to form a new version of the band. One of their first gigs together was alongside the Rolling Stones at the City Hall in Sheffield on 13 November 1963. They did OK, but it was never the spark of the original Big Three or the Flamingos. By April 1964, Paddy Chambers had left the band to play with the Dominoes in Hamburg, before teaming up with Gibson Kemp, John Frankland and Lewis Collins (who played Bodie in *The Professionals*) to form a band called the Eyes. Collins left the band and later played bass with the Mojo's, before taking up an acting career. Frankland left and Chamber and Kemp brought in Klaus Voormann on bass and became Paddy, Klaus, and Gibson. Faron, meanwhile, left the Big Three in the summer of 1964.

He once again formed a band named the Flamingos and continued to thrill an audience with his stage routines. However, during the last years of the sixties, he went under the radar. The beginnings of a family had started for the prancing prince, who took employment in the 9 to 5 society. By the mid-1970s he had answered the call of the stage and once more formed a new Flamingos band. He accepted an offer to go over to France from Vic Wright. In France, they steadily built up a fan base as the gigs came in. Faron was earning good money but homesickness forced him to return to Liverpool. That sickness passed quickly and he was soon back out among the French. This time he was playing with a band named Blue Suede and they turned out to be hot property as the bookings for gigs and festivals flew in. Faron also hosted his own radio show while in France. Life, and the money, was good. However, when his mother fell ill Faron wanted to return to the UK to be close to her.

Based back in Liverpool, Faron reignited the Flamingos and continued to thrill audiences with his lively performances. The band members came and went and included such names as Brian Jones, Arty Davies, Phil Melia, Mike Rudd, Billy Burton, Arthur Hayes, Nicky

Crouch, Phil Berube, Albie Donnelly, Ken Shalliker, Bernie Rogers, and Owen Roberts, among many others. Faron became involved with the Merseycats charity and has performed many countless times over the years to help their great cause. He has appeared at Merseybeat events that have taken place within Merseyside and around the country. Faron is a very welcoming man who is happy to chat with fans and pose for photographs.

In the early 1990s, Faron suffered a heart attack. It was the first of many, which, along with a serious throat operation, have eventually led to him having to retire from performing, although he will still make the odd appearance from time to time at a charity event and give the crowd a song. He has recorded a number of CD albums, including *Faron 2002 – Raining In My Heart, My Dream Songs* (2013), and *Let It Be Me* (2016). If you manage to have a chat with him you will see that he remains as lively as he ever was.

Faron is a legend of the Merseybeat scene and is one of the most recognised characters from that era. He is up there with Rory Storm for stage presence and entertainment factor and, just like Rory, Faron was years ahead of his time in those early golden years of the '60s.

Faron on stage. (Courtesy of Mave Atherton)

The panda-footed prince may have been grounded from prancing and dancing, but that smile and the laughter remain.

The Koobas

Formed in 1962, they consisted of Ray Morris (lead guitar), Keith Ellis (bass) Stuart Leithwood (rhythm guitar), and John Morris (drums). The members had joined from two bands: the Midnights and the Thunderbeats. The band's first name was the Kubas. They played the local scene before venturing out to Hamburg in late 1963 to appear at the famous Star-Club. On their return, they caught the attention of Brian Epstein, who signed them in 1964. The band were given a part in the film *Ferry Cross The Mersey*, though the scene that featured them playing was omitted from the final cut. Their first single 'I Love Her'/'Magic Potion' was released by Columbia records in January 1965, though it failed to make an impact. The group now altered the spelling of their name to 'Koobas'. The guys were booked by Butlin's for the summer season at their camp in Ayr, Scotland, before returning to the studio to record. Their second single 'Take Me For a Little While'/'Somewhere In The Night' was released by Pye in December 1965. The release coincided with the band joining the Beatles for a short UK tour between 3 and 12 December (the Beatles' final UK tour). During a performance at the Liverpool Empire, the band was joined on drums by Paul McCartney for their version of 'Dizzy Miss Lizzy'. The publicity of the tour failed to push their single and it never reached the charts. Two singles released in 1966 also missed charting: 'You'd Better Make Up Your Mind'/'A Place I Know' and 'Sweet Music'/'Face', though both are decent recordings. The band was now moving towards the psychedelic music. The year 1967 started with a performance in London alongside the Who and the Jimi Hendrix Experience. However, their two singles during 1967 again failed to chart. The brilliant version of 'Sally' B-sided with 'Champagne and Caviar', and 'Gypsy Fred' with 'City Girl'. The following year saw them tour Switzerland with the Jimi Hendrix Experience; a tour that led up to their single, and another wonderful cover: 'The First Cut Is The Deepest'/'Walking Out'. The publicity, however, once more failed to generate the interest of the public. Then, the band went into the studios at Abbey Road to record an album called *Koobas*. It was released in 1969, but by then the band had split. It never took off big for the guys, but they played alongside some of the biggest names in the business and left us with some really great recordings.

Violet Caldwell

Here is yet another lady who was years ahead of her time. Vi had an incredible energy to encourage and back her children in everything that they did. She instilled a belief in them that they could achieve anything that they set out to do. Her children, already talented, simply flew with her backing. Iris became a dancer, stage actress, and spent time as a redcoat at Butlin's. Alan took up dancing before showing his skills as a sportsman. He excelled in athletics, so much so that he was considered for competing in the 1960 Rome Olympics. Then the music took over, and he became one of the best frontmen every to come out of Merseyside when he co-founded the Hurricanes and became Rory Storm. Let us not forget Vi's husband, Ernie, who also backed his children in every way that he could.

Vi had a profound influence on many of the people that she met. Her amazing zest for life touched not only the friends of her children but also many of the musicians who became the well-known names of that era. The Caldwell home became a meeting place for many of the Merseyside music family, who named her 'Ma Storm'. After gigs had finished, many people would pop into the house to relax and enjoy the company as well as the endless supply of tea and chip butties. Vi could beef up a performer and encourage them, though she could just as easily bring down any inflated ego. It was all about the banter, friendship, and encouragement of everyone. People who were visitors still speak highly of those wonderful nights sitting among friends as Ma Storm held court over a kettle and chip pan.

The Beatles were regulars at the house that Rory had christened 'Stormsville'. They loved Vi, especially Paul and George, who both grew close to her – it was Vi who told them to smile after their first TV performance, telling them that they would never get anywhere with miserable faces. These two Beatles never forgot the Caldwell family and returned to visit whenever they could. George still came until around 1968, and Paul right up to 1970.

Vi Caldwell gave the musicians a place to relax and connect with one another. She basically managed the Hurricanes in their early days and gave a shoulder and encouragement to a number of musicians whenever they needed it. She is remembered fondly and spoken of in high esteem by those who knew her.

The Caldwell family: Ernie, Iris, Alan, and Vi. (Courtesy of Iris Caldwell)

Karl Terry

Karl is one of the great legends of the Mersey sound. He was born Terence John Connor in Liverpool on 10 March 1942. His career started when he was aged just fourteen as a member of the Gamblers, who sometimes went by the name of the Teen Aces. The band also featured Les Braid, who went on to play bass with the Swinging Blue Jeans. The year 1957 saw the band change its name to Karl Terry and the Cruisers, and go on to become a very popular local outfit. It has been reported that for a short period a number of the members of the band played under the name the Wolfgang Combo. Karl was christened 'The Sheik of Shake' by Bob Wooler for his onstage antics. On 19 October 1961, the Cruisers played a gig at the Litherland Town Hall alongside the Beatles and Gerry and the Pacemakers. During the evening it was decided that a single supergroup could be formed to thrill the audience. The Beatles and Pacemakers joined forces, with Karl leading the band on vocals. They played under the name of the Beatmakers for this one night only. By 1963 the Cruisers had decided to call it a day. Karl played with the Delameres before going on to front the TT's. He then joined the T Squares and spent time working with them in Germany. By 1966 Karl had begun to play bass and guitar with Rory Storm and the Hurricanes. However, when the Hurricanes guitarist, Ty Brien, passed away in February 1967 the band split. Karl had served his time as a bricklayer and could easily have returned to that profession, though the lure of the music was too much for him and he decided to reform the Cruisers.

The band has continued to play at home and abroad with members coming and going. Karl, however, remained at the helm with his exciting stage show. He toured the US army bases in France during the 1960s and played his part in the Merseyside Hamburg invasion. Karl has returned to Hamburg many times over the years to perform and entertain. He must have played with almost every Merseybeat icon, as well as touring with such profile names as Tom Jones, Sandie Shaw, and the Rolling Stones. In Liverpool, he is known as 'Our Karl'. The city is proud of this very humble and friendly man who has entertained so many for so long and who remains a pleasure to sit in company with. If ever a man loves to do what he does best, it is Karl Terry.

It is a complete mystery how a performer of such quality as Karl did not record until 1978, which was when he and the Cruisers appeared on the album *Mersey Survivors* with the song 'I'm Gonna Be a Wheel Someday'. The band also recorded a single called '2 Hound Dogs'/'Sea Cruise', though it was never released. The song 'Cruisin' was recorded around this time too but was not released either. That same year, they also released the single 'Haunted House'/'Stick It In Your Pipe' under the Rox label. During the 1990s, Karl and the band recorded the album *Rock 'N' Roll – That's All*. Karl has also recorded a number of CDs over the years and appeared at most of the main Mersey sound events at home and abroad.

What is impressive in Karl's story is the way he has stayed loyal to the music that he loves so much, from the rock 'n' roll songs to the suede shoes and Teddy-boy drape jackets that he performs in whenever he goes up on a stage. This guy loves doing what he does and that comes across to an audience. Karl remains performing to this day with his fellow Cruisers and is a sight to behold as he moves from hand-waving dance routines to leaps through the air that finish in full-on splits. Remember, this is a guy in his seventies; he is still an incredible showman with a great voice. It is very simple, if you read or hear that Karl is playing somewhere close to you then go along and see him. If not, then you are missing out on an authentic Merseybeat act that still thrills and rocks an audience.

Karl Terry. (Courtesy of Mave Atheron)

Arty Davies

Many people have it tough and face barriers during their times playing in bands, though very few will come up against the daunting obstacles that Arty Davies not only faced but conquered in his music and life. His parents,

Lillian and James, had lost their first two children shortly after birth, so when Arthur Henry was rushed away for a blood transfusion moments after his birth on 13 April 1948, their fears must have been immense. However, little Arthur pulled through and went on to thrive.

Aged around eighteen months, Arty became very ill with fever and aching muscles. He also had slow reflexes and was suffering from bad headaches. After a number of days the doctor spotted that he was in fact paralysed, and rushed him to Alder Hey Hospital. Once more, Lillian and James had to sit and wait in fear for the news on their child. Finally, they were called into an office to meet with three doctors, who informed them Arty had poliomyelitis and that he would never walk again. After a few moments of stunned silence, Lillian told the doctors 'he will walk' and left the room. Arty was fitted with leg callipers that hurt him. His parents bought him a bike that would help strengthen his legs and Arty rode it everywhere. The outcome was that Arty began to walk and proved the doctors wrong.

When he was aged five, Arty was admitted to the Myrtle Street Children's Hospital for a hip operation. This left him in an almost full-bodied plaster cast, which stretched from his ankles to just below his chest. He was treated terribly at the hospital: he was ignored and left to soil himself in bed, then staff would wipe faeces on his face when he did it. He was a small boy around some very nasty people. When Lillian found out she went nuts and took him home. Another orthopaedic specialist said that he was disgusted by the way the operation had gone and called the surgeons and doctors who had treated Arty 'animals'. He was now operated on at Broadgreen Hospital, where he stayed on a ward full of men and was spoilt rotten.

He walked again and in October 1962 he almost flew when he saw the Beatles for the first time on TV. A few weeks later he watched the band the Notions perform at a school Christmas party. He was now hooked and began to go along to the Cavern to watch the bands. He loved it, and it was the Undertakers who really blew him away more than anyone else.

A polio Christmas party at the League of Welldoers, off Scotland Road, saw Arty and a few friends daring each other to do things. One said that he was getting up to sing with the band that were playing and Arty said he would play the drums. His friend backed out but Arty got up there and played along to their version of 'Money'. Arty saw his friends goading him to hit every drum but he ignored them and tried to stay with the band. Afterwards, the band suggested to him to take the drums up. A very excited Arty told his parents about his playing and how he wanted a set of drums; however they did not believe him and told him he would never be able to play the drums because of his disability. He was so upset – once more obstacles had been put in his way.

His parents did agree to buy him a Tuxedo bass on HP from Hessy's. He joined the Rapides, with the lads teaching him the bass lines to their songs. On 24 April 1965, Arty made his one and only appearance with the band at the Blue Union club in Window Lane, Garston. He was scared stiff but the lads covered him. He played another gig with a few friends and although probably awful it was also fun.

Arty hated playing the bass and an accident, although painful, was about to change everything for him. He was practising with a friend when suddenly an enormous electric shock from the bass guitar threw him across his bedroom and straight into the wardrobe. Luckily enough his pal managed to pull the plug out, which probably saved his life. His parents were shocked to find that he had almost died and said 'that gear is going back'. Come Monday, Arty was at the Hessy's shop based in Stanley Street. Frank Hessy agreed to exchange the equipment and Arty said: 'I don't want another bass. How about a set of drums? You don't plug them into the leccy'. His parents agreed and they opted for a second-hand Premier white pearl set. After two years of asking, Arty had finally got his drums. The Pressure Points were his first real band, followed by Korner Kafe, though both bands petered out. After a few audition failures, Arty lost heart and started to drink. He was slipping into a dangerous situation and needed something or someone to bring him back out.

It was two old friends who dragged him back when they turned up and asked him to play wheelchair basketball. At first he refused, but then decided to give it a go. When he did he was a natural, and it led to a forty-two-year career within the sport. His first club was Liverpool, then South London Aces, North London Hawks, and then Southport, with whom he won two European Champions. He also played for Great Britain and was first British player to score a winner against the USA. Arty went on to Start Runcorn Raiders and helped a number of players to go on and play for the Great Britain Men and Women teams. He played for Oldham Owls, then coached Liverpool Greenbank, Wolverhampton, and Leeds Spiders. He also coached the North West Under 11s and the Under 19s, who never lost a match.

Basketball had given Arty a new lease of life and helped him back to his first love of music. He started playing again with the Gibson James Band before joining the Bandanas, then the Early Years, who later became the Four Just Men; Flashback was another group that he was involved with.

Arty was asked to join Lee Curtis & the All Stars, which he accepted. They played a few shows before Lee decided to leave the band, who stayed together under the name of Roadrunner. Next it was Luke Warm and the Radiators, before later joining the Tempo's. He was also by this time involved with the Merseycats charity, where he would play during events. One day at Merseycats, Faron Ruffley walked in and everyone asked if he was making a comeback after his heart problems. He replied, 'Yes! And that's my drummer,' while pointing at Arty. Just like that Arty was now a Flamingo. Faron and the Flamingos played most of the Merseybeat events, where they thrilled the crowds. Arty also played with a band named BAD and when Faron played with them they were called F and Bad.

One day he answered his phone and was shocked to find Ted 'Kingsize' Taylor on the other end asking him if he would sit in with the Dominoes for their gig at the River Festival show at Wallasey Ferry terminal. Arty accepted, after all this was one of his dreams. Arty loved every moment of it and he went on to sit in with the band on other occasions. He also played regularly at the Sound of the '60's Sunday gigs at the Cavern Club and has been a member of both the Merseyrats and Lanky Kats, who both perform for local charities. He became a member of the band the Knight Crew and sat in with the band that had thrilled him as a youngster in the Cavern Club, the Undertakers.

The list of bands that Arty has played with goes on and on. Arty has come through so much and has not only achieved his dreams but has blown each goal apart. He is proud of his music, sport and of his association with Faron Ruffley – the two guys became firm friends. Arty remains a valued and well thought of drummer. Not bad for a kid who had so many obstacles to face.

Denny Seyton and the Sabres

Denny (Brian Tarr) formed the group in 1963. They entered – and won – a Battle of the Bands contest and were rewarded with a recording contract with Mercury Records. They were tipped for success, though their first single, 'Tricky Dicky'/'Baby What Do You Want Me To Do', released in January 1964, failed to chart. This was followed up in May with 'Short Fat Fanny'/'Give Me Back My Heart', though once more nothing came of it. In August 1964, they released a third single 'The Way You Look Tonight'/'Hands Off'. This song got them into the charts, where they peaked at No. 48. Wing Records, a subsidiary of Mercury Records, asked the band to record an album made up of covers from recent hits. They took up the offer and It's The Gear was also released during 1964. The LP featured songs such as 'Can't Buy Me Love', 'The Hippy Hippy Shake', 'Just One Look', 'All My Loving', 'Not Fade Away', and 'Needles and Pins'. The guys were offered a percentage of sales or a lump sum of cash for the album; they took the cash. The band played at the Star-Clubs in Germany and at one time had Lally (Harold) Stott as a member. Lally, though described by some as a bit crazy, went on to write the smash hit 'Chirpy Chirpy Cheep Cheep', which was a hit for the band Middle of the Road, spending five weeks at No. 1 in the summer of 1971. Lally, born in the Prescot area of Liverpool, was killed in a motorcycle accident near his home in 1977. The band was signed by Parlophone to record a single. They changed their name to the Denny Seyton Group and released 'Just a Kiss'/'In The Flowers By They Trees' in late 1965. The single, however, did not chart. The played on through a number of member changes until finally calling it a day once more. They have reformed a number of times over the years for charity events.

The Hideaways

John Donaldson, John Shell, and Austin (Ozzie) Yue, were school friends at the Liverpool Institute. Excited by the outburst of the thriving music scene within their city, they decided to try and form a band themselves. Yue sang and played guitar, Shell played bass, and Donaldson was on drums. By the start of 1964 they had been joined by Frankie Connor on rhythm guitar. The guys practised and set about finding somewhere to play. On Red Cross Street, opposite the Albert Dock, stood a coffee bar that hosted groups called the Hideaway. The lads went in to talk to the owners and told them that they were a band called the Hideaways. They were given a gig and impressed so much that they were handed the offer of being the resident band. For the next few months they performed there on a regular basis, until Bob Wooler approached them and brought the band to the Cavern Club. The lads wanted to improve their sound and placed an advert in a local newspaper for a saxophonist. It was answered by Judd Lander, who informed the guys that he could only play the harmonica. However, Judd was very good at playing it and fitting into their rhythm and blues style, so he was in. Being a resident band at the Cavern led to them being chosen to be filmed playing at the club for a TV advert about Timex watches, so they were on the telly all the time. They were a seriously good band who gained a decent following.

During 1965, two Dutch people approached the band and the Clayton Squares about a book they wanted to write on the music scene in Liverpool. The book *Beat In Liverpool* was released in Dutch and German. It contains some amazing photographs of the two bands, fans, and venues. Accompanying the book was a live recorded EP. The Clayton Squares were recorded at the Cavern, while the Hideaways performed 'Black Night' and 'Momma Keep Your Big Mouth Shut'. Both tracks were recorded at the Sink Club.

John Shell had married Elaine Curtis, and in the summer of 1966 their daughter Amanda Jayne was born. No recording contract came for the guys, despite them sending around demos. It would appear that the Merseyside bands were now losing their appeal to the record industry as they pushed on for a new sound. More fool them, as they missed out on a lot of talent within the area. The band continued and began to play further afield.

John Shell, who had been born in Arkansas, Dallas, had come to Liverpool aged two with his Liverpool-born mother. With him still holding an American citizenship, he was drafted into the US Army. Of course, he could have argued the case that he was a British citizen and fought to stay in that country, but he decided that it was his duty to serve his birth nation, even though he knew it would take him into a war. The band agreed that Dave Collins would step in to help the guys out while John was away.

John arrived in Vietnam on 1 December 1967 and was posted to Quan Loi for training. Here he undertook a two-week course in jungle fighting, known to the troops as 'Jungle Devil School'. John served as Private First Class, 11B10 Infantryman, with C Company, 1st Battalion of the 28th Infantry Regiment, 1st Infantry Division. He saw action in the Binh Duong Province during January of '68. On 31 January 1968, John was sent into action around the An My village to counter-attack the enemy's Tet Offensive. Sadly, he was killed close to the Phu Loi airfield, which was being used by the US Army. John's death was listed as 'Misadventure'. A friend who was serving with him told of how friendly fire was mistakenly aimed towards them as they made their way to fox holes after landing on the airstrip. It appears that the soldiers manning the guns had not been given word that back-up troops were landing and had mistaken them as part of the

John Shell and his daughter Amanda. (Courtesy of the Shell family collection)

enemy attack. John was killed during this action. His body was flown to the UK for burial. Six US soldiers carried his coffin, draped in the American flag, into Anfield Cemetery. A gun salute was given before a lone bugler sounded 'Taps'. John is the only person in the world to have a brick on both the wall of the Cavern Club and the Washington Memorial. A number of years back his daughter, Amanda, posted a very moving internet tribute to the father that she never really knew.

The band had to carry on with the knowledge that John was never coming back. Dave Collins stayed with them and they continued to go down well and draw a crowd. Ritchie Routledge, from the Crying Shames, joined them on vocals during 1968 when Judd Lander moved to London to pursue his career. In 1969, RCA signed the band up to produce a single. Their name was changed to Confucius, with Ritchie Routledge leaving along with Dave Collins, who was replaced on bass by Chris 'Fingers' Finley. In early 1970, their single 'Brandenburg Concerto (That's What It Was)' was released. For the B-side, they recorded 'The Message'.

The band carried on for a while before the members decided to split and follow other careers. They played at the Cavern Club more times than any other band and are rather proud of that record. John Donaldson retired from full-time music. Frankie Connor went on to become a DJ presenter for Radio Merseyside. Ozzie Yue joined the band Supercharge who became very popular at Liverpool's Sportsman Bar in the mid-1970s. He toured and recorded with the band, who had a No. 3 chart position in Australia in 1977 with their single 'You've Gotta Get Up and Dance'. He also played in the Liverpool band Joker. Ozzie became an actor in the 1980s and has appeared in many productions on TV and stage. He later performed with his own band You Who. Chris Finley went on to play with Herman's Hermits and the Merseybeats. Sadly, he passed away in February 2016. Judd Lander went on to play as a session musician with some of the biggest names in the business. Have you ever wondered how so many pop bands have a great harmonica player on some of their tracks? Well, that is Judd, doing what he does best.

The guys have reformed a number of times for special events, including the Mathew Street festival in 2009. They have never forgotten their old friend John Shell, and always dedicate a song to him whenever they perform with the words 'this one is for John'. Frankie Connor, along with Alan Crowley, wrote the song 'A Poor Boy From Liverpool' in his honour. The band did record the songs 'I Wish You Would', 'But Not For Me', 'The Times I Wish', 'I Know What You're Thinking', and 'Life's a Drag', but they were never released. In March 2017, the band reformed for an emotional gig at the Cavern Club in memory of Chris Finley. They had less than an hour of rehearsals together, yet they still blew the Cavern audience away with their fantastic set. These guys remain what they always have been: absolute class.

Ivan Stax (Ayub Ali)

I was looking for a story to include in this book that would give an insight into what it was like for a youngster to be inspired by the Merseybeat bands enough to start performing themselves. I found that story in Ivan Stax. However, it is not just Mersey sound artists who inspired him, but those from within his own community of Liverpool 8.

He was born at No. 191 Windsor Street, Liverpool, in 1949. His parents were Frances Jones (who was born in Bancroft Street, off Upper Parliament Street, in Liverpool) and Romjan Ali (who had been born in Bangladesh, India, and had come to Britain in 1923). Romjan had given his children Muslim names that he thought sounded like the English names he and Frances had chosen. So, although his birth certificate says 'Ayub' he was known as 'Ivor'. Romjan had served with the merchant navy. During the Second World War two of the ships that he was sailing on were torpedoed, with the second incident leaving him with chest problems until the day he died. Ivor can still recall how his father would sometimes have awful nightmares and shout out in his sleep as he was taken back to those horrific events.

His parents ran several shops, with the main one being on the corner of North Hill Street and Windsor Street in the Liverpool 8 area. It was called Ali's 12 O'clock shop but was usually open until around 2 a.m. Ivor attended Upper Park Street Infants School. His mother had him converted to the Roman Catholic faith at the mission in Great Georges Street. In his final year of education at Mount Carmel the school closed and Ivor spent that last year at St George's school off Mill Street.

Around 1953 Ivor heard 'Shot Gun Boogie' by Tennessee Ernie Ford playing on the family radiogram and was drawn to the music. Then he heard Wynonie Harris singing 'LolliPop Mama' and 'Don't Roll Those Blood Shot Eyes At Me'. Ivor was hooked. To him, Wynonie was the originator of rock and roll crossing over from rhythm and blues. While watching movies at the local cinema he discovered Fats Domino and Little Richard and described these moments as 'WOW!' By 1957 Ivor had discovered the song 'Momma He's Making Eyes at Me' by Johnny Otis that featured Marie Adams and the 3 Tons of Joy. It blew him away, and his love towards music was sealed. He also fell for Helen Shapiro in both looks and voice. Cliff Richard was the darling of the British charts as the '60s began but he just did not cut it with Ivor, who had no idea what he wanted but knew that something must surely change. That change came in late 1962 to early 1963 when four Liverpool lads burst onto the music scene. And when they did, they changed everything: the music, the dress, the way of thinking. This was what Ivor had been waiting for.

Ivor attempted to put together a group with around ten other lads. This new 'biggest band in Liverpool' consisted of a number of guitarist and Ivor on a drum kit made from steel drums and biscuit tins. The band soon finished as most of the members realised they were not very musical. Ivor, however, was hooked and kept practising on his put-together kit. His brother Ronnie played guitar and had banned Ivor from ever touching it, though he still snuck into his room to play it upside-down (he was left handed), saying, in his own words, 'I made a noise'.

Another of his older brothers, John, was a very good singer but with awful timing. One night in 1964 he got up with a group in the Flat Iron pub on Mill Street. He had the voice, the confidence, but no timing. The band later knocked looking for John to play a gig in with them. With John unavailable, his mum said, 'Our Ivor could do it.' He agreed, though his confidence was lacking. The next night the Mersey Blues Preachers called to pick him up for a rehearsal at a house in Old Swan. In Ivor's own words: 'I was f*cking awful and as my shyness kicked in. I felt sorry for those guys.' When he arrived back home, he stayed up all night learning the lyrics of the song set. The next day he waited near his home to be picked up. However, they never showed.

Ivor managed to persuade his father to purchase an Olympic drum kit for £80 on HP from Bradleys in Lord Street. He took a car wash job in Park Lane to help make the payments. One day, a guy approached him and asked if he was a drummer. Ivor told him that he kind of was, and the guy asked him if he would come along to Stanley House that evening to try out for a band, to which he agreed. Ivor joined the group, who consisted of three brothers: Ralph, Alan, and Roy. Without any PA system, they would rehearse in Ralph's bedsit at No. 27 Canning Street.

The Nigerian Social Club gave them a freebie gig and someone turned on the jukebox while they were performing. The next was an audition at the Merseyside Artistes Club in Sheil Road, where they were introduced as the Buzzie Ben – again, they died. Ivor recalled one night while rehearsing in Stanley House: 'I could hear a guy sat near the stage singing along so he was asked to sing on the mic and blew everyone away, it was Bernie Wenton.' The band asked Bernie to join them but he declined and the band split them up a short time later. One thing Ivor did take from it all was his friendship with Bernie Wenton.

Ralph from the band contacted Ivor about starting to gig with him on bass, a guitarist, and Ivor on drums. Things went well and they even got their first paid gig from Odie Taylor at the 21 Cafe in Great George Street for £9. They did OK until the guitarist received a borstal recall. Ivor took a job with the family coal business, which was hard work but decent money.

Ivor's skills really started to shine when he traded in his drum kit for a Thomas organ. He would spend every night during 1967 playing the organ to records – mostly the Beatles and Stax, Atlantic and Motown releases – just learning and learning. Sometimes he would stand in Harry Brown's butcher's doorway with a few friends singing Beatles and doo-wop songs. In early 1968, he was stood on the corner of North Hill Street and Princes Road when Alan Sef, Silver Chantre, and Willy Wenton (aka Randy King) came over to say hello. They were in a group called the Shuffler Sound and asked Ivor to come and jam with them. After the session, he agreed to join the band if they performed more Motown numbers. Two days later, they played at the Pyramid Club – the old Iron Door Club. It was not a good performance but not a bad one either. The band struggled with decent equipment and van drivers. Alan Williams

Ivan Stax working at the family shop in Windsor Street, Liverpool. (Courtesy of Ivan Stax)

was helpful, giving them five or six nights a week every now and then at the Blue Angel Club for £10 a night. Mick Kearns came in on saxophone to enhance their sound, while Willy began singing more like Otis Redding.

Ivor's oldest brother Kenny, who lived in Peckham, London, came along to watch them play at the La Bamba on Prescot Road. He was impressed and told them that he could maybe get them a week playing in London. Kenny booked them into Cam Records by Moorfields station for a four-song demo. Ivor was very disappointed by Cam, who seemed to just want their money. Kenny took the demo to London and a few days later phoned up to say he had three gigs booked in Peckham. It was great and they were offered more work, meaning that the summer of 1968 was spent down in the Old Smoke. It was a valuable experience and great fun, though various issues – musically and personal – saw the band return to Liverpool.

Willy and Ivor formed the group again, with Tony Goldby coming in on bass. Tony had a van so he was certainly welcome. They persuaded Mick Kearns and Silver Chantre to return and added Phil Howard on drums. One of their favourite venues to gig was at Reece's in Clayton Square. It was while playing here in the February of 1969 that they found their missing link in the shape of Bobby Wenton, who was a great vocalist and a tremendous showman. However, Silver Chantre decided to leave not long after.

In early 1969, Ivor met a lady name Maria Porcelli, who he became rather smitten with. They soon began dating and within a short period had become a perfectly matched couple. The band became very popular, with every gig a storming success as they had gained an enormous following. Playing five or six nights a week for very good money, they could do little wrong. However, a few of the band members wanted to turn pro and travel. Some did not and, with no regular drummer, the band split once more.

They reformed (again) in August 1969. Billy Good came in on bass, with Alan Sef on drums and Bernie Wenton joined to give them three vocalists. Les Martin came in on bass before Albie Donnelly joined on tenor sax. The band were doing great at this time, but for Ivor somehow the spark had gone with so many changes and he decided to move on.

In early January 1970, Ivor was asked, and honoured, to join the In Crowd. They were the most popular group in Liverpool at that time, although by then they very rarely performed in the city, mostly playing on the north-east cabaret circuit and over in Northern Ireland. They were a great band who had a single out and earned good money, but Ivor just felt like an outsider. He stayed for a few months before deciding to leave. He was done with groups and gigging and settled into a humdrum job in his parent's corner shop. He hated it and would spend most of his time on the parlour piano composing songs.

In 1971, the music had called out once more to Ivor, who teamed up with Willy Wenton, Tony Goldby, Mick Kearns and Phil Howard to form Stateside Review. They produced really good arrangements and harmonies, though they packed it all in after just a few gigs and Ivor returned to the corner shop. He then joined the Main Attraction, the band of his younger brother Danny, who also included Eric Cornwall and Tommy McCann. When Danny was spotted by a talent scout for the record producer Tony Hall and signed up, the band brought in Mick Kearns and Dave (Gaffa) Silvera – two tenor sax players. Within weeks they were producing a very good, tight sound. Ivor was taking all the lead vocals and soon lost his voice. There was no more falsetto, just growling and Barry White, but they got by and did well gigging. In 1976, Ivor and Maria were married. Mick left to join Karl Terry and the Cruisers in 1977. After that, members left one by one.

By 1982 Ivor had packed it all in and took up driving a Hackney cab around the city. He also joined the Equity Actors Union, though was informed that the surname 'Ali' would hold him back from TV work.

Main Attraction. (Courtesy of Ivan Stax)

He decided on the stage name of 'Ivan Stax'; 'Ivan' as many people mixed up his name and called him that, and 'Stax' for his love of Stax records. However, he dislikes the name Ivan, so we shall continue with calling him Ivor. Bumping into Tony Goldby on Lodge Lane led to a jam session that was pretty good, so the two guys decided to form an act. They called themselves Grapevine, found a few gigs, and slowly their fees got bigger and bigger.

The compère at the Montrose club suggested they should enter the Whitbread Entertainer of the Year competition. Ivor laughed, but Tony, who had more belief, suggested that they should do it. They cruised through to the semi-final, where they were up against their old Shuffler Sound mates Bernie, Bobby, and Willy Wenton, who were performing as the Buzz Brothers. To their amazement, they beat their pals to reach the final, which consisted of some great acts including the Blaize Brothers, Bobby and the Crescents, and the comic Denny Waters. Tony had always said 'believe in yourself', and this belief paid off when Grapevine were announced the winners. The prize was £1,000, and the following day a nice write-up about the duo appeared in the *Liverpool Echo*. It also led to an invitation to perform in Church Street as the Liverpool Christmas lights were switched on. Then in April 1986 came a two-week booking in Palm Beach, Los Americas, Tenerife. It was an absolute success and the guys loved their time there.

They remained semi-pro and Ivor became sick of driving the taxi cab to make ends meet. When he was offered some solo gigs and extra work in *Coronation Street* he took it and split from Tony. He and Maria had a baby on the way so the work, along with Ivor performing as Ivan Stax in a solo act, would provide a good income for the family. Maria and Ivor went on to have two children. Ivor has remained a solo artist who still performs around the country today. He went on to include Neil Diamond and Barry White tributes shows into his act.

In 1999, Ivor and Sugar Dean enrolled on the course Instrumental Music Facilitator (IMF) via the Leicester-based group Access to Music Ltd. They both completed the course, which basically consisted of home-based work alongside two days per week teaching in schools – in Ivor's case, Oldershaw in Wallasey. The Labour government set up the programme New Deal for Musicians and Ivor, along with Sugar, was hired as a music industry consultant having unemployed musicians referred to them. If they were up to the task he would refer them to LIPA as part-time students for one year. Ivor became the north-west

Ivan Stax. (Courtesy of Ivan Stax)

regional manager for two days a week in between teaching as an IMF at Ridgeway High School in Birkenhead. He spent several hours at LIPA every week checking that his students were OK. The government shut down the scheme in 2006. Today, Ivor remains performing as a singer and working as an extra in *Coronation Street*.

8

The Beat Keeps Going

The music of those early Merseyside days still remains popular. One of the reasons for this is likely because the musicians and singers loved to do what they were doing. Almost sixty years since many of these performers first started out on their musical paths, a number of them are still playing – now that is dedication. In Liverpool you can see a number of performers playing and mixing at two clubs: the Oldy club in Aintree, the host for the Merseycats, while the Lathom Hall is the home of the Merseyrats. Both are charities that have raised a lot of money for sick and deserving children within the Merseyside area. Other musicians and singers from the '60s era can be found playing at pubs and clubs across the area. Fort Perch Rock in New Brighton has been hosting Merseybeat events for many years, while the Cavern Club is another place where you can still find '60s legends performing at times. Across the country and around the globe, the lads and girls who created that special sound can still be found up on a stage. They are a truly talented group of people. These musicians and performers have inspired a generation of artists to replay the music of those wonderful days. Many 1960s-sounding bands have sprung up to play the popular hits, others have shaped themselves around the live acts that had thrilled so many, while some have gone far out of their way to recreate the original sound. We are still provided with the music that refuses to lose its popularity, and long may it continue. Let us take a look at a few of the performers who were too young for the Merseybeat but who clearly have a desire to play the music from those times that has inspired them so much.

It was 1982 when the author of this book boldly took the steps down into the Beaconsfield pub on the corner of North John Street/ Victoria Street. After finding a corner to hide in, he would only have a coke as he was terrified of being caught drinking underage. After a short while, a noise erupted. It was the band of the evening bursting into their set. People jumped up to dance, others sang along, and that under-aged coke drinker came out of his hiding spot to explore the sound that he was hearing. With immediate effect, he was hooked, transfixed, and tapping his foot along. This was nothing like anything he had heard before. This was excitement, brilliance; this was Mojo Filter. Of course, he had seen numerous '60s bands playing at pubs and clubs that he had snuck into. But, these guys! They were the real deal. They simply blew him away, and he started to follow them around on a regular basis. They were friendly guys who had a wonderful loyal fan base, and many friendships were formed that last to this day. So, it is only right that I start with the band that put the beat into the author of this book.

Mojo Filter

In 1979, Paul Cooper and Andy Hudson decided to form a band, with the driving force being to recreate the energy of the music on the Hamburg tapes, which they found intoxicating. Andy began to learn the drums and Paul was on guitar. Both guys travelled over to Birkenhead when Andy bought his drum kit and they carried it all back on the underground train. Other members of the band included Tim McGrath and Steve McGann, though Steve could not play his bass guitar he just held it. They practised at the St Anthony of Padua social club in Mossley Hill and had their first gig at a student bar at Christ College, where Andy was studying for his degree. The gig went well and after a few more they decided that they needed a bass player who could play. Actor Mark McGann joined the band playing rhythm guitar and Paul switched to bass as nobody else could play it.

As with most bands, members chopped and changed. Eventually, they came to the classic line-up of Phil Melia (lead), Paul Copper (bass), Rick Alan (rhythm), and Andy Hudson (drums).

They played the local circuit, where they quickly gained a large following. Of course, the bookings took off as promoters eagerly booked this popular band who became regulars at the Beaconsfield pub as well as Daley's Dandelion and the Cumberland Tavern. Their appearance at the Beatles conventions at the Adelphi Hotel went down fantastically with the audience, and had Bob Wooler saying across the

Mojo Filter. (Courtesy of the Mojo Filter collection)

microphone that he had not seen a reception like that for a band since a certain foursome back in the 1960s.

So, why were they so popular and sought after? First of all, they were very, very good at what they did. They were also not a tribute band, as many others were. These guys played the classics and the rare songs that the Merseybeat sound had been built upon. They also included a number of '60s numbers that had been hits for bands around the world. However, and most importantly, Mojo Filter never tried to copy any artist; instead, they played it their own way and the sound that they produced was authentic and full of spirit and energy. If you never managed to get to see them play live then you missed out on something really special. The band played 376 gigs during 1981. This was possible by sometimes playing a pub and then a club on a Friday, and then doing an afternoon gig on the Sturday followed by a pub and a club. As with any band playing that number of gigs, it helped them to become musically very tight and hone their unique sound.

The guys were beginning to be tipped for big things. A number of recorded tracks were played on local radio and a fan club had started, with great success. Their talents were not restricted to cover version as was illustrated when they struck a deal to release a single with

Chiswick Records. 'All Of The Time' was the self-penned single, with another of their own compositions 'I Told You' filling the B-side. The single sold locally among their loyal fans but the label was not big enough for it to get near the national charts. It is a great song and readers should seek a copy out to listen to.

The year 1984 was one that saw so much happening for the band. Royal Life Assurance had overseen the rebuilding of the new Cavern Club and Cavern Walks development. They had used Mojo Filter during the promotion of the new Cavern and the band was invited to play at the opening night on 26 April 1984. In fact, the lads were the first band on stage that evening and kicked off the music with Phil belting out 'Talkin Bout You'. They had also sneaked almost forty people into the event by hiding them in the back of their van – but

The single 'All Of The Time'. (Courtesy of the Mojo Filter collection)

ssshhh, that is a secret! Watching the band that night were Pete Best, Walter Eymond, Cynthia Lennon, John Gorman, and Mike McGear, among others. The thing that stunned everyone was the fact that the entire club had been carpeted; something that would never last and, sure enough, the quickly stained and smelly carpet was gone within months. What does sadden the author is despite the guys playing the Cavern that opening night and on many other occasions, along with being a part of the promotional side of everything, no brick bears their name on the wall of fame outside the club. That is rather shameful and something that hopefully will be rectified in time.

A week after the Cavern gig they played at the opening of the Liverpool garden festival on 2 May, with Mark McGann joining them for the gig. The band had made people sit up and notice. The sheer excitement of their performance had brought the interest from outside of the city. The offers were beginning to come in and Mojo Filter were about to spread their wings.

Phil left the band for a while and Brian Peters stood in as the guys flew out to take up an offer of playing in Hamburg. Just like the Beatles and other Merseyside bands had done back in the day, they played

Mojo Filter. (Courtesy of the Mojo Filter collection)

from 11 p.m. to 6 a.m. playing half an hour on, then half an hour off – they loved it. The first night that the band played the club was selling bottles of Grolsch for 8 marks. They were told that they could buy them for 3 marks as they were the band. The lads kept buying them and selling them on to the punters for 6 marks, thus making a profit and getting free drinks. The club ran out of bottles that night and the following evening the band was informed that their drinks would now cost them 5 marks as their scam had been found out. With Phil back, they went on to tour Japan, Holland, Germany, Italy, Belgium and the UK. They were a very popular band who thrilled audiences wherever they played. While in Japan, they were offered a recording contract that involved them staying out there for the next six months. As with another certain band, they all had to unanimously vote on any decisions that they had to make. One member did not want to stay in Japan, so back they came. All things must pass, and it was a sad moment for their fans when the band finally called it a day. However, these talented boys were not just going to lie down and be forgotten.

They have performed together a number of times over the years, including from 2011–2015 playing together as Mojo Filter at the Cavern Mecca reunion gigs. Phil Melia went on to do sessions and

Mojo Filter at the Cumberland Tavern, Liverpool. (Courtesy of the Mojo Filter collection)

projects with various bands including the Ruthless Rap Assassins (EMI), Mind, Body and Soul (Polydor) and Jimmy Cauty (the KLF). Jamming is his passion and he was delighted to take the chance to jam with Les Paul in New York City. He was also a member of the Shakers and appeared on most of their recordings. He later toured and recorded with the Pete Best Band. Paul Cooper went on to play with the brilliant rock-based band Sliced Bread before performing as Paul McCartney in the Bootleg-Beatles band. He later got a band together called Broken Wings, who performed Wings and Beatles songs and were absolutely amazing. Rick played with a few bands in the short-term, including a comedy-themed group called the Crackpots. He then performed as George Harrison with the Cavern Beatles, with whom he toured the world. Rick married Maria in 2013 and, along with his musical abilities, he has turned his attentions to his love of photography, with stunning results. Andy retired from music after Mojo Filter split. As he says, 'When you've been in the best, why play with the rest?' He managed the Cumberland Tavern too, where the guys had proved extremely popular for two years before moving to Essex. He met and married Mary and they had four children together. Andy started up his own successful business selling computer software around the world. The Mojo reunion gigs must have enlightened something in Andy for, in the last few years, he has joined a rock-styled band called the Power Band.

With Mojo Filter it really comes down to that old saying 'you had to be there'. The excitement and electricity that this band created was incredible. These guys were not just a great talent, they were also down-to-earth approachable guys who socialised with those who followed them. Basically, they created a Mojo family that those who were lucky enough to be a part of still look back on with great fondness. Wonderful times indeed.

The Shakers

When I first saw the Shakers play it was just like those early days of the 1980s when I set eyes – and ears – upon Mojo Filter. They just blew me away. I have been fortunate to have seen the Shakers perform on many occasions, with each time being as thrilling as the last. The guys in the band are very approachable and friendly. There are no big egos, they just love doing what they do best. Tony

O'Keeffe is a first-class drummer who has played with a number of bands throughout his career. He also 'trod the boards' as an actor, and has been involved with the theatre both on stage and behind the scenes. His passion for Merseybeat music has been with him since his childhood, and his love of the beat bands is clearly there for all to see. His desire to play the Mersey sound music was heightened during the 1980s with the opening of the new Cavern Club. Tony was quick to get himself playing on the club's stage.

He was intrigued when he purchased an album by a band called the Rapiers. They were a London band who played beat music more authentic than he had ever heard from a modern band before. A number of books and plays about the Mersey music also fuelled his wish, though his commitments with other bands left him unable to give it serious thought. Not that it bothered him then, it was just not the right time as he explored other musical routes. During the 1990s, Tony took a holiday in Butlins; there, providing the musical entertainment, was the Rapiers. He could not believe what he was seeing as he watched the band play. They just blew him away. He had never seen a '60s group live that was so authentic in sound, instrumentation, and appearance. He wanted to do this too! He did play some '60s music for a few years around the local circuit, though it was more of a general thing than being strictly beat. Tony continued to tour with a number of bands, and it was during this period that he came across another fantastic and authentic '60s band in the shape of the Scottish outfit the Kaisers. Once more, his desire to play this music arose in him.

Back in Liverpool, Tony became the musical director for a theatre show about the Merseybeat period. It featured a live band that performed original songs as a backing to the story they play. Tony made sure that the band looked and sounded right. There was a huge energy about the group being set in that period. For Tony, the desires were awoken once more, and this time he acted upon them. Of course, being Tony, he was thorough in everything that he did. He researched the idea, testing if it would work out. It was a gamble – after all, he had to still make a living – and he could have easily been excused for taking the option of 'stay as you are'. Musicians are self-employed and sometimes that safety net of current work is enough to make a person think that the risk of going for their ambition is just too big. However, Tony has a 'do what you gotta do' attitude and he was more than ready to take up the challenge.

From day one, it was all about the original look and sound. Although he admires such bands, he wanted something different from the '60s groups playing around the pubs and clubs. It was not a tribute band that he wanted to create, but an authentic, raw energy the '60s Merseybeat group performing a show as the originals had. The clothes and instruments were just as important as the music to Tony. Probably his background as a theatre musical director played its part in shaping the band's look and sound into the style of those early days. As he says himself: 'It always struck me that theatre sound, in musical plays I'd seen etc. was more authentic when coupled with the period setting. The bands in the shows always sounded different than the ones playing regular venues.' Members were sought, practice sessions held and, once he was happy with the outcome, the performances were ready to begin.

A number of names for the band had been discussed before the idea came to Tony. He approached Ted 'Kingsize' Taylor to ask if he could use the name the Shakers, which Ted and the Dominoes had used as a false name to record an album with Polydor records while still signed to another company. Ted gave him his blessing and the name was set. It was of great importance for Tony to keep the band's set to Merseybeat music. He dug out a number of the obscure B-side songs and researched the live sets that the bands back then had played in Merseyside and Hamburg. He now had an authentic set list for the band.

The Shakers first took to a stage at a private function in Gloucestershire in late September 2005. A few weeks later they made their Liverpool debut with a gig at the Olympia Theatre. Soon after that, they descended the steps into the depths of No. 10 Mathew Street to make an appearance at the Cavern Club. The popularity of the band rose very quickly and they soon had a good following. Promoters wanted to book them, including for the Cavern, where their authentic style and sound fitted so well. They were playing a slot at the club every month.

When Ted 'Kingsize' Taylor and Wes Paul started the regular Sunday slot 'Sound Of The Sixties' at the Cavern, the Shakers could be found playing at the event on many occasions. Here, they would find themselves jamming with musicians and backing singers from those early days of Merseybeat. This was a real honour for the band, as well as a vital learning curve that would only enhance the authentic sound. As the years passed, band members chopped and changed, though the sound and look remained of a high standard. By 2009 the

Tony O'Keeffe with Ted 'Kingsize' Taylor at the Cavern Club. (Courtesy of Wes Paul)

Shakers had taken up a regular Saturday slot at the Cavern Club, with a weekly Thursday spot at the Cavern pub opposite. So popular were the band that the Cavern Club eventually swapped their Thursday at the Cavern pub and gave them a residency at the club every Saturday and Sunday.

The Shakers at Fort Perch Rock when Phil Melia was with them. (Courtesy of Mave Atherton)

Today, the band still spends the weekends thrilling the locals and tourists down in the Cavern. Of course, they play gigs elsewhere too. In fact, their portfolio is a very impressive read. They have performed all over the UK, Europe, the Middle East and the USA. They have played at the International Beatleweek in Liverpool since 2006, along with appearances at Beatles festivals in Belgium, Switzerland and Italy. The band performed at Ostend's Paulusfeesten festival and has given headline gigs in Bahrain, Belgium, Germany, Spain and Jersey. The year 2013 saw them blowing the crowd away when they debuted at the Beatles festival Abbey Road on the River in Kentucky. The list of stars they have backed is very impressive indeed and includes, among others, Tommy Roe, Chris Montez, James Burton, Tony Sheridan, Mike Pender, Billy Kinsley, Terry Sylvester, Beryl Marsden, Nick Crouch, Geoff Nugent, Kingsize Taylor, Karl Terry, and Lee Curtis. The Shakers have had their own theatre show tour across the UK, as well as playing many 1960s music events.

The year 2010 saw the band recording the EP *Cavern Stompin*, which consisted of the popular Cavern songs 'Some Other Guy',

The Shakers in the recording studio. (Courtesy of Andy Sandler)

'Slow Down', 'Bad Boy' and 'Roll Over Beethoven'. Their second EP *Mach Schau!* came out in late 2011 and features four songs associated with the Star-Club in Hamburg: 'Rock 'n' Roll Music, 'Red Sails In The Sunset', 'Besame Mucho', and 'I'm Gonna Sit Right Down and Cry (Over You)'. In 2014, the band recorded an album with Soundflat records called *A Whole Lotta Shakers*.

They have also appeared on the compilation albums Soundflat *Records Ballroom Bash! Vol. 8*, and *Dynamite No. 43 – 20 Years Of Rock And Roll*. All of their recordings feature the three guys who play in the band today: Tony O'Keeffe, Eddie Harrison, and Martin Davies. They also include Phil Melia, who was with the band back then. The Shakers remain a thrilling live band that continues to entertain and thrill an audience.

The final comment on their story should go to Tony O'Keeffee:

The lineup has changed many times over the years but these things happen, things change over long periods of time but we always carry on with business as usual. Professional standards apply. While we weren't the first to do so in the UK, I think we certainly helped bring the 'authentic beat' thing back to Liverpool, and indeed The Cavern, again at least. [Not counting the original guys who invented it and are still

The Shakers at the Cavern Club. (Courtesy of Pat Trish Jones)

rockin' in a lot of cases, I'm pleased to say] Our collective cap is always doffed to the original beatsters in Liverpool who paved the way and I'm so glad that we've had the opportunity to play with many of them and still do. Sadly, some of our Mersey beat brothers have now departed, so we will continue to fly the flag for those who rocked and rolled in the beat clubs and dance halls of Hamburg and Liverpool. The beat goes on.

Victoria Jones

In the shape of Victoria Jones, Liverpool has produced yet another talented lady to show the boys that they cannot have it all their own way. She began her career as a child dancer. She graduated to being the first one up on stage for karaoke during family holidays. She was also a huge fan of Kylie Minogue and would get her mother to curl her hair so that she looked like her idol while she belted out her songs. By the age of fifteen Victoria was performing on the local cabaret circuit. She clearly had a talent for the stage, and upon completion of her GCSEs she informed her parents she was going to enrol on a performing course. Her father's reply to that statement was 'I don't think so,' as he wanted her to complete her A-Level exams and find a good job. However,

Victoria had her mind made up and enlisted herself onto a BTEC Performing Arts course at Southport College. The course consisted of singing, dancing and acting, and she sailed through it, gaining many leading roles during performances. Her abilities also led to her being recruited to appear in pantomimes. As her popularity grew the need for demo recordings arose, and it was her parents who helped her achieve this. Her father had once played five-a-side football on a regular basis with Billy Kinsley from the Merseybeats and it was Billy who recorded Victoria's very first demo tracks for her. She felt very honoured that someone of Billy's calibre was prepared to do that for her.

At the age of eighteen, Victoria joined a three-piece band called the Force, who would travel around social clubs playing the popular chart hits and old favourites. When the opportunity arose she took a job for two years at Disneyland Paris. While here, she sang the cast members' theme songs, which were recorded and broadcast across the resort a number of times every day. She also appeared in 'Mickey's Show Time' and 'Lilo and Stitch's Catch The Wave Party'. Victoria was also employed as a backing vocalist for contestants on the popular French TV talent show *Star Academie*. Having such a love of the stage, she also joined a country-themed girl band in France called the Rodeo Girls. Once back in the UK she continued to act, dance, and sing, and toured as a Kylie Minogue tribute under the title of 'I Should Be So Kylie'. Not only did she sing like Kylie but the act included many costume changes to give it the real feel – for those now wondering: yes, those hot pants were included.

In 2007, Victoria was involved in a car accident. This left her to contemplate her life and she decided to follow her dream. When the BBC advertised for contestants to appear on a new talent contest named *The One and Only*, Victoria applied to appear as Kylie Minogue. She made it through her heats all the way to the finals and although she did not win the show, it was a fantastic experience for her. Of course, it highlighted her act and the bookings came in. She appeared as Kylie all over the UK as well as many times overseas. Victoria was also voted the UK's No. 1 Kylie tribute act.

Victoria had been raised by parents with a huge love of 1960s music so it is hardly surprising that this is the direction that she has decided to venture into during her career. In her own words:

I love the sixties sound, the raw edge of it all and the raspy, powerhouse voices of Lulu and Tina Turner, I love soul and Jazz and I think I was

Victoria Jones outside the Cavern Club. (Courtesy of Jamie Dannunzio)

born in the wrong decade. I am a fan of the early Beatles music and love all the head shaking that goes with it.

She has built a great reputation performing on the circuit, singing the classics of some of her favourite '60s artists including Lulu, Cilla Black, Tina Turner, and Dusty Springfield among others. It has also been of huge importance to Victoria to look the part of the music that she sings. This has certainly come across through the authentic dresses that she wears while performing and goes right down to her hair, make-up, and jewellery. This lady also has no fear towards taking on the songs of the Beatles and the top 1960s male performers. She will happily sing them in her act as she shows the guys that the girls can do them just as well.

The jobs have come in for this very talented lady with a bubbly character, and she has appeared in a number of musical productions including *Escorts the Musical, Heart and Soul,* and *The Meatloaf Story,* as well as showing us her wild side in the musical *Vampires Rock.* She also appeared as Anna in a *Frozen* tribute show. It is very easy to see why she has been cast on many occasions to play Cilla Black, though she will tell you outright that she is not a Cilla tribute act. If anything, her tribute is to all the female singers of the 1960s who she admires so much. Funnily enough, at the time of her interview for this book she had just completed a UK tour of the stage show *Cilla and the Shades of the 60s,* which has received fantastic reviews.

Victoria was fortunate during the tour to have her backing vocalists, the Shades, comprise of her close friends Anna Slater, Emily Clarke and Nicola Twardowski. They have all performed together on numerous occasions and have many funny stories that they may tell you if ever you are in their company. Victoria has shared one story for the book:

> Me and the girls were once asked if we would consider performing at a private function as the Spice Girls. We thought "that could be fun" and agreed to the gig. After a short practice and the obtaining of costumes, we were ready to entertain and turned up at for the performance. What had been failed to be mentioned to us was that the function was for a funeral, and it all seemed a bit strange as we danced around the stage singing teeny-bopper classics.

It is a joy to watch Victoria perform the songs from the 1960s. She really has a tremendous ability to deliver each song in a very authentic style and transfer the listener back to those glorious days. It clearly

Victoria Jones at the Cavern Club. (Courtesy Jamie Dannunzio)

comes across just how much she loves to perform. She is a very lively and funny person, though very humble with it. While being interviewed for this book she was asked where she would like her career to go and her reply was typical of this very down-to-earth girl: 'I just feel so very lucky to do what I do.' There is very little chance that the work is about to dry up for this amazing singer, who will continue to thrill and entertain the crowds wherever she performs. Hopefully, big things are around the corner, although, to be fair, she already is a star.

TAXMAN

The magic of Merseyside and its performers reared its wonderful head in 2012 when a group of Italian guys had their dream come true: performing the Beatles' music at one of the venues that the Fab Four had once played at in Liverpool. The gig had been arranged between Geoff Nugent and Beatles guide Stevie T. Turner, who runs the Mop Top Tours. The band TAXMAN consisted of Giorgio Stiriti (lead guitar), Antonio Chila (rhythm guitar), Enio Peritore (bass guitar), and Pino Lo Giudice (drums). Their friend Stefano Musolino had also travelled with them from Italy to film their performance and take photographs.

Italian band TAXMAN, with Geoff Nugent. (Courtesy of Pino Lo Giudice)

Pino recalled the event:

Basically, it was Stevie-T who arranged our gig at the Lathom Hall. He had approached the one and only Geoff Nugent (God bless him) and had kept me in touch with him. It was Geoff who had proposed that we play at the hall on August 30th. We received a very warm welcome and were treated like real rockstars. It was a great experience for us all. Geoff has given his guitar to Antonio to play, while David Morgan passed his guitar to our lead guitarist Giorgio. As I am left handed I was changing the drums around so that I could play them when I was stopped by a gentleman who has told me 'Please, you are our guest, don't worry, I'll change the drums for you,' he left me speechless. The gig was fab, everyone was singing and dancing and had fun. After the show we talked (and drank) with many Mersey beat legends including Lee Curtis who sang an acapella version of Elvis Presley's 'Teddy Bear' with us, we enjoyed it all so much. I was honoured to play 'There's a Place', which is my favourite Beatles song, in the town that I fell that I belong to.

Author's Note

It was as a schoolboy in 1979 that I first decided to venture up Mathew Street to see where Rory Storm and the Hurricanes had played. Yes, I was a Hurricanes fan. The Beatles would have to wait another year or so until the senseless murder of John Lennon for their attention to be brought to me. As I walked along the street that very first time I was left wondering where had everything gone. The club Eric's was there, but I was still a few years away from realising just how important a venue this was and that one of my favourite bands, the Teardrop Explodes, were playing there. However, that is another story. I discovered that the ugly flat piece of land being used as a car park was, in fact, the site of the former Cavern Club. I did wonder if someone had been winding me up, as I thought to myself 'how the hell can anything have ever happened here?'

Sadly, in the late 1970s, Liverpool was not the Beatles or Mersey sound attraction it is today. There was very little in the city to remember those incredible days. A trickle of tourists would arrive looking for the club where the Beatles had been discovered. What they found was a car park and an almost deserted Mathew Street. Those who knew their history would venture into the Grapes or White Star pubs, before heading off to the city outskirts to visit the Fab Four's homes. In fact, the only Beatles-related items for them to see in Mathew Street were the Arthur Dooley statue, standing high up on a wall opposite the car park, and the former cavern sign. Many of the musicians would still be plying their trade, though it did appear that Liverpool was forgetting its own history. However, two people were determined to keep it all going.

Liz and Jim Hughes were two Beatles fans with a passion for remembering the band that they loved and the music of the Merseybeat era. They first set up the Magical Mystery Store at No. 24 North John

Street in the late 1970s. On 3 January 1981, they moved into the premises on the top floor of No. 18 Mathew Street (above what is now Flanagan's Apple). Here they opened the Cavern Mecca – the first ever Beatles museum in Liverpool. The tourists now had somewhere to visit when they arrived at the street, though it also became very popular with the locals as well. Bob Wooler, Uncle Charlie Lennon, and Eddie 'The Walrus' Porter could all be found here at times (and in the Grapes pub). Eddie worked at the Cavern Mecca and later went on to become one of Liverpool's favourite Beatles guides. The Mecca was the forerunner of what was to come.

Liz and Jim were also responsible for organising a number of Beatles conventions, with the first one being for the August bank holiday in 1981 at the Royal Court Theatre. However, the theatre suffered flooding so the Adelphi hotel stood in at the last moment. The hotel hosted the conventions of 1982 and 1983 before Liz and Jim opted for St George's Hall for the 1984 event. By April 1984 the newly built Cavern Club had opened its doors to the public. Not long after,

Liz and Jim Hughes. (Courtesy of Pat Trish Jones)

the Cavern Mecca had to move premises into the newly constructed Cavern Walks. It was never the same, and within eighteen months the doors had closed for the last time. Sadly, Liz passed away in 2008.

There were bars, statues, the wall of fame, shops, the No. 1 disc wall and even a hotel. Mathew Street is now a major tourist attraction and a hive of activity. Of course, it was all very different in 1981 when Liz and Jim opened the Cavern Mecca. None of the tributes in the street mention their name, but they really should. Hopefully, time will see recognition for this wonderful couple, who kept it all going when others had cried enough.

Another person who I would like to mention is Miss Mathew Street herself – and my mate since we were kids – Julie Sudbury. Not only is she a friend to everybody, but is also a remarkable and kind person who does so much for so many.

In 2011, Julie decided to organise a reunion for former Cavern Mecca members to come together again and celebrate the 30th anniversary of the museum. At first she doubted her ability to get something so daunting off the ground but little by little she began

Julie Sudbury with her partner Tony O'Keeffe.

to make contact with people, and was stunned by the response. Not only were they excited to attend such an event and meet up with old friends, but bands and celebrities were happy to give their time as Julie had decided to use the reunion as a charity fundraiser. The evening proved to be a complete success.

The reunion has grown so much over the last few years that it now takes place in the Cavern Club lounge. Performers old and new gladly give their time to an event that has become one of the most anticipated occasions of the year: The brilliant Hamburg Beat, the Shakers, the Gardens, Mojo Filter, the Media, Cavern Mecca Babies, Hub Flashback, and the Rockets. There is always a mishmash of bands formed just for the event, which contain youngsters alongside old pros, and actors such as Michael Starke and Andrew Schofield. Paul Codman performs a fine job as compère and keeps the mood happy with a good laugh along the way, not forgetting Pat Trish Jones, who produces stunning pictures of the evening in between making everyone giggle with her crazy antics. It is a wonderful event that has raised thousands for charity. Many people give so much to make the event

Some of them there actor types giving their time and a great performance for the Cavern Mecca do. (Courtesy of Pat Trish Jones)

the success that it is and they should all be thanked, as should those who attend.

As for Julie Sudbury, she never seeks the credit for what she has achieved. Not only in terms of fundraising but for bringing so many old friends back together. Well, Julie, so many are grateful for everything and proud to be your friend. On a lighter note, and as the author of this book found out through experience, never be sitting on your arse in the Cavern band room when Julie comes in wondering why things have not been done – I moved very fast, ha ha! Keep up the great work Julie.

Of course, without the performers who brought us the music, we would have no books to recall these magic times. We thank each and every one of them who made this all possible when they took to the stages and provided us with something truly special that has lasted for so many years – and shows no signs of stopping. Let us also not forget the club owners and promoters who provided the settings and events that helped the music grow and change history. What happened either side of the River Mersey from the late 1950s onwards really was magical, wonderful, talented, and downright incredible. Remember it with enjoyment and pride, and keep on enjoying the magic that is the Mersey sound.

Acknowledgements

I would like to thank the following people: Mave Atherton, Margaret Byrne, Wes Wilkie, Ted Taylor, Mary Dostal, Sylvia Wiggins, Val Gell, Tony O'Keeffe, Julia Sudbury, Pini Lo Giudice, Carol Philips, Victoria Jones, Ramon Sugar Deen, Larry Wassgren, Joey Ankrah, Mandy Falkingham, Elaine Shell, Ivan Stax, George Dixon, Garry Christian, Jimmy McGrath, Ozzie Yue, Frankie O'Connor, Karl Terry, Mikey Rogers, Suzanne Hogan, Sam Hogan, Mark Atherton, James O'Hanlon, Mike and Ree Callan, Melissa Wenton, Gaz Wato, Pat Trish Jones, Mojo Filter and everybody else who has helped me in any way with this book. Without you I could not have produced it – thank you!

All photographs within this book carry details of ownership beneath them. Any that are not marked this way are ownership and copyright of the author.

Disclaimer
Every effort has been made to identify the photographer(s) and/or copyright holders of all illustrations in this book. If information and credits have been overlooked, the author requests the copyright holder to make contact with the publisher to ensure proper credit in all future editions.